Country Turnrows

Best Wishes,
Jim Steiert

Contents

Introduction xi

Trim Around the Edges 1
In Praise of Pocketknives 5
Trace Elements 8
The Sole Saver 10
Working Logic 14
Rhyme by the Road 16
The G-Man 19
Things Work Out 21
Elevator View 24
Communion 26
Hoe Hands 33
Tractor Music 36
Hog Scaldin' 39
Livestock Teaches Life 43
Courage and Sportsmanship 45
Elephant Ears 48
Looky Here 50
The Great Spring Break Fishing Fiasco 52
Like a Wave on a Slop Bucket 55
As Silly As... 57
Home Remedies 59
Windmill Adventures 63
Instant Replay 65
Francie's Bread 69
Pie Power 72
Country Cafes 74
Batchin' Hotcakes 78
Ears of Summer 81
Scent-Sations 83
Comfort Food 86
Small Town 88

The Folks Behind You	90
Catch You Next Time	93
The "Old Cranks"	96
Soil Science 301	99
Ten-Speed and Tylenol	101
Danger: College Move-In	104
Endings and Beginnings	107
Great Horny Toads	110
Goose Tales	113
Beadie, the Goose Hunter	116
Horse Sense, Dogies, and Dogs	119
Politics Goes to the Dogs	123
A Tale of Two Turkeys	126
Tilth and Tomatoes	129
Dawn and Dusk Magic	132
Weather Signs	134
Wind: The Trial of March	137
Hail, Hell, and Rainwater	139
Scare Holes	141
Randy's Roundup	144
Hay, Hold the Hard Drive	147
Tradin' Pickups	149
Following Precedent	153
Irrigated Irony	155
History's Perspective	157
Red-Top Cane	160
Indian Summer	162
Bracing Days	165
Wondrous Rituals	167
Picking the Corn Patch	169
The Blessing Of Surplus	171
Farmyards and Pumpkins	173
Fall Orange	175
Inside A White Cow	177
What Is It With Mamas?	180
Easter Is For...	183
A Few Daddyisms	186

Country Christmas Eve	188
The Messenger	191
The Cowboy Camp	196
Keep It Simple, Stupid	201
When Christmas Went to the Dogs	204
A Wrinkle in the Twinkle	208
Following the Stars	211
Coming Home	214

Introduction

Somewhere back in ancient times man got the bright idea that he could farm more country if he harnessed an ox or a donkey to a wooden plow.

Shortly thereafter he discovered that when he got to the bottom end of the back 40 he would have to turn beast and tillage implement around, or he would plow into the Tigris, the Euphrates, the Nile, or the adjoining olive grove of the one old sorehead neighbor.

The area where he pivoted the plow was the first turnrow. It was useful enough for turning around and as a boundary between fields.

Its true utilitarian function, however, was that it provided a space where he, and one of the several friendly neighbors plowing across the way, could pull up their oxen abreast, take a pull from the water bag, lean against the plow, pick their teeth, and chew the fat.

"Howdy, neighbor. How much rain didya' get?"

"Oh, we caught a good shower down on the other end of the place, but only about enough to wet a jackal's whisker on this side."

"Well, we got a sprinkle, too. Some rain beats no rain. Least it didn't hail. Whatcha' gonna' plant this year?"

"Dunno. Maybe some barley for loaves ta go with fishes. Loaves and fishes are hot right now."

"Ya' checked the barley and fish futures?"

"Naw, that's all fixed by the pharaohs, anyway."

"How much seed barley ya' gonna' put out?"

"I figger' a handful every couple steps will work—long as I scatter most of it on good soil and don't get too much in the road or the shallow or rocky ground."

"Didja' hear that Pharaoh Farm 2 is plowing with four-oxen-drive now—and they've beat some old swords into plowshares too—they can get across a good part of an acre in a day with that kind of power."

"Wonder how bad their fuel bill will be, running those big red hay burners?"

"Gosh, little guys like us can hardly afford a wooden plow and one ox. We got no chance at all against those corporate pharaoh guys.

Guess we're gonna' hafta' get big or get out."

"What kinda' locust treatment ya' gonna' use this year?"

"Well, I hope we don't have a plague. I'm bullish on wild honey—gonna just gather plenty of it. If the locusts eat my crop I can at least eat them—long as the honey holds out."

"Gonna' fertilize?"

"Yeah, the ox is just sorta' scatterin' it as we go."

"Well, I've let old Ferdinand cool down enough. Guess I better get him movin' and finish this next through before dark."

"Okay, neighbor. Ya'll come."

"Yep, ya'll, too."

Across the centuries from two yoke of oxen to four-wheel-drive, the turnrow has remained an agrarian commons, anchored in functional practicality as a listening and gathering ground.

If you want to blame the pages trailing this introduction on something, observation, maybe a little folklore, and turnrow experiences may all be held at fault.

Truth be known, I am a farm kid who has spent his share of time sitting on pickup running boards, leaning on fences, tractors, grain trucks, and combines, or with an elbow cocked out the pickup window, listening to tales and philosophy as presented in agrarian turnaround zones.

For me, summertime tractor driving stimulated ideas and internal discourse—once I mastered the challenging movements of turning the M Farmall at the end of the field while dragging a Hoeme with sweeps.

Plowing back and forth from one turnrow to the other, pulling a Hoeme, a disk, or a cultivator was the price of keeping constantly-growing weeds from overrunning the farm.

The long intervals of plowing were thought-provoking times of pondering and daydreaming on all sorts of wild story lines.

As I grew up on the farm both severe hayfever and the peculiar compulsion to write were in me. This pollen-plagued plowboy became a parlayer of paragraphs.

Folks told me that I would outgrow it—I think that they meant the hayfever. While I am still waiting to outgrow the misery, I take pills—that don't help all that much—for the sneezes, sniffles, and watery eyes.

The writing compulsion, I fear, is beyond medicating.

Over a span of years I have done full-time staff work for two newspapers, corresponded for two more, "stringed" news for radio and television, worked full-time and as a free-lancer for *The Texas Farmer-Stockman* magazine, free-lanced for outdoor magazines, including *Texas Parks & Wildlife* and *Texas Sportsman*, and wound up writing in a public relations role for West Texas Rural Telephone Cooperative.

All of this has allowed me to keep company with farmers and ranchers all over Texas. Through the years, first at *The Hereford Brand*, and later, in the *Co-Op Connection*, the newsletter of West Texas Rural Telephone Cooperative, I've chronicled some of my thoughts in my "On the Turnrow" column. A sampling of those are compiled here, along with assorted other efforts.

Sadly, a magnitude of us have left our rural roots and become urbanites. Too many have forgotten the once-close link with the land and the sense of community.

Just about two percent of our country's population feeds the other 98 percent. This logistical accomplishment could loosely be likened to what Matthew, Mark and John recorded about what the Lord did with a few barley loaves and fishes.

Rural America's feeding of us all, both physically and spiritually, and the rooted-in-the-soil rural way of life has near-religious implications, accomplished, as it is, with no little degree of grace from the Almighty, and faith on the part of its practitioners.

If, God forbid, the country ever goes hungry, we will suddenly think a lot more of the "two percenters" than we apparently do now. Stockmen, plowboys, and country folk carry on, unpretentious standard-bearers of a deeply-ingrained work and service ethic. I don't think folks come any finer than those from the country, small-town places.

When a farm sale is coming up, the auctioneers mail out handbills. Sale items are listed under headings such as tractors and implements, toolbar makeups, panels and livestock equipment, farm trucks and pickups.

Stuff that doesn't fit any other category gets thrown together in "lots." ...One lot of grease guns and grease cartridges... One lot of hand tools, shovels, hoes, axes, and post-hole diggers... One lot of logging chain... One large lot of rowbinder parts and twine... One lot of fence post and railroad ties...

...Here is one lot of plowboy/stockman/rural life essays, ramblings and such, along with one large lot of odd thoughts put down in print after they were farmed and formed in journeys between country turnrows.

Trim Around the Edges

You not only get a trim, but grooming in humor, news and fellowship in this bastion of rural life.

The rural pulse can still be taken down at the barber shop. We don't mean those snotty, reservation-a-week-ahead-of-time-only "styling salons." We're talking a real barber shop, where you drop in unannounced—except on Mondays—no barbering on Mondays. You take your chances on how many folks will be ahead of you in line and you wait your turn.

Some days, especially Fridays and Saturdays, the place is going to be packed. Other days, you can walk in and sit right down in the big swivel chair, or only have to wait for a couple of folks ahead of you.

You are greeted by barbers with names like Perry or Ronny or Billy, Shorty or James. They pause over the head of hair they have in disarray, scissors or electric clippers poised in one hand, a comb in the other, a howdy and a possum grin at the ready. A gallery-in-waiting sits amidst the thumbed-through newspapers, farming, sports, fishing, hunting and American Legion magazines, one knee cocked over the other. These guys are good for howdies all-around, the latest one-liners and Aggie, lawyer and politician jokes that get lumped together by their nature.

Gallery members comment on how the guys in the barber chairs are going to regret the scissor-wielding of the proprietors. They volunteer to run the clippers themselves when an especially deserving "friend" is in the chair.

If some poor fellow is getting a little thin on top, the gallery remarks about the barber getting carried away with his cutting... Thin-haired fellows deserve a discount. We with "layout acreage" up top don't have $10 worth of hair in the first place.—About the only thing that is going to get clipped is our pocketbook.—Barbers claim that they ought to charge us a discovery fee, just for finding a strand or two of hair that is long enough to trim.

Anybody coming in the barbershop door is fair game for humor. I heard a veteran beat everyone to the punch recently. "Good morning, gentlemen," he remarked. "Oh—and you barbers, too," he wisecracked.

A few years ago a fellow in a barber chair said he hung his Christmas tree upside down. We were all trying to figure that out when Shannon Hacker Redwine, a nice-looking young lady who is the sister of one of the fellows down at the telephone co-op, and who was single at the time, came into the shop. She went right up to the guy in the swivel chair, gave him a big hug and asked if he was going to hang his Christmas tree upside down again this year so that she could come see it?

When she left, chrome-domed Perry the barber went into a frenzy. Hair was flying. The guy in his chair finally pleaded for Perry to take it easy.

"I just want to hurry and finish up so I can get right home and hang my Christmas tree upside down," Perry reasoned.

For the price of a haircut you get to climb into the barber chair and become an expert on any subject... at least for the fifteen to twenty minute duration of the clip job.

There have been more fine fish caught, more big-racked bucks dropped, more district football, basketball, super bowl and world series games won, more baseball and football pots raked in, more political solutions arrived at, more crops and money made from the lofty heights of the barber chair than from any stream or lake, forest, field, government hall or market.

We sit in sock feet in the barber's chair while the shoeshine-man-in-residence restores scuffed boots to glistening life over in his corner that smells of boot wax.

Our conversation is accompanied by the buzz of the clippers, the snick of the scissors around our ears, the warmth of shave cream, the rhythmic stropping of blade against strap, followed by nerve-testing scraping of the straight razor at the nape or our necks.

Talk arrives not so much at how things are, as how they ought to be. If the masses out there would just listen to the uncommonly good humor and sense spoken by barber chair sitters, we might not have to worry with trivial things like crime and the national debt.

"Resident observers" usually drop in daily down at the barber shop. They take up choice seats on the street-side window ledge or near the gumball machine by the door. These "color commentators" gather news, remark to the barber on lopping off the ears of young squirmsters, then give pennies to the same so that they can slug the gum machine, offer sage advice on history and making it through hard times, ruminate on weather signs, recall who married whose sister, detail who farmed the old Nanny place in '06, tell secrets of how to keep borers out of the peach trees, recall skinny dipping.

If the establishment remains a classic tonsorial parlor, these resident observers may even take a bite out of a plug of tobacco and make use of brass spittoons on the premises.

Patrons rotate, barber chairs swivel. Talk traverses lineups, injury reports, big plays, huge players, who looks tough on the schedule and whether the local boys can play up to their potential, or why they didn't. We hear about the shortest route to the lake, how best to catch the fish in it when you get there, and the best way to cook them up if you are lucky enough to catch any. Sometimes, barbers allow the conversation to degenerate to the level of golf, but most times, try to keep the truth-stretching on a higher plane.

Depending on the season, talk may turn to planting, stands, how many times have you cultivated, when will you start irrigating? Big crop, or no crop on account of a hailstorm. When is this hot, dry spell going to break? We sure do need a rain. How much was in your gauge? Sure hope it dries up so we can harvest. What kind of winter do you look for? How much hay are you feeding? Are the winters getting colder? When is this one going to end? I remember one worse back in...

Talk is of how income taxes, school taxes, county taxes are all too darned high. It's all the fault of those damned politicians and lobbyists, how we ought to be taking care of home folks instead of gallivanting off in some foreign land.

Everything wrong with the country is due to the sins of the Democrats, the Republicans, Congress. The farm bill is, as usual, all screwed-up; the working man has to hustle just to scrape enough together to live at the poverty level; how Charlie's son in the Army over in the drifting dunes just made sergeant and we are all mighty proud of him; how J.D.'s granddaughter sure looked cute in that picture on the front page of the paper the other day.

Conversation is of *let's pick our shifts and buy our tickets for the Lion's Club, Kiwanis, Rotary, Red Cross, Boy Scout, FFA, 4-H, Booster Club carnival, chili dinner, burger fry, pancake supper, cake walk, pie auction, pheasant hunt, garage sale, and raise some money for the volunteer fire department, ambulance service, hospital, disaster relief, Girls' Town, Boys' Ranch, old folks home, stock show, field trip, scholarship fund.*

It is of *did you hear about good old Joe? He has been real sick, and he is a fine fellow with a family to support and we sure think a lot of him. His poor wife has a hard row to hoe while Joe is getting better... We'll get some tractors together tomorrow and get over there and get their plowing caught up.*

The chairs in the gallery empty and fill again, quickly on the busy days, less so on the slow ones. Barbers hear a few new stories, especially when a customer who hasn't been by for a while drops in. They gather bits of news and hear the latest jokes, many of them over and over again. The barbers are PR men enough to keep right on laughing at the punchlines. Country barbers probably would not make bad diplomats—surely no worse than career politicians.

The little towns and the farm communities and the friendly barbershops smelling of shave cream and tonic water, hair slickum and boot wax, sadly diminish in number.

We who are lucky keep on coming back, ostensibly for hair grooming, but also to be groomed with humor, news and fellowship in one of those rare establishments that reflect the soul of our rural communities.

When the barber removes the lap cloth, brushes the loose hair from our shirt, lowers the pumped-up chair and takes our payment, he always tells us to "hurry back."

He knows that we have good reason to—even if we only need "a trim around the edges."

In Praise of Pocketknives

Pocketknives, pliers, and "Texas lacing leather" are essential make-do instruments.

The pocketknife is numbered among requisite tools for life in the country. Give a rural person a pair of pliers, some "Texas lacing leather" (baling wire), and a pocketknife, and they can make-do and keep the machinery of the world running.

Names like Buck, Gerber, Case, and Old Timer ring with honest utility, bespeaking instruments of utter practicality—steel ground to the fine edge of durability.

A pocketknife becomes a treasure of boyhood. When you are a little guy standing in on the spit-and-whittle sessions of the Dads and uncles and neighbors, you feel excluded if you do not have this essential tool to pull from your pocket, so that you too can work on a stick or poke in the ground.

I can still remember the first pocketknife I had. It was a miniature job with a single folding blade and the logo of the local cotton gin on the side. The blade was difficult for young hands to open. The assistance of a Dad or some other adult figure was required. This speaks well of the good sense of whoever made them.

"Old Shep," the late Roland Shepard, and his late wife, Rosa, gave the little pocketknives to customers of their cotton gin at Hart. The Shepards obviously gave due consideration to the wishes of five-year-old farm boys when deciding on patronage favors for their customers.

The little pocketknives were just the right size to fit in the small pocket of a kid who had previously been left out when Dad and the big guys were skinning back a stalk of redtop cane or stirring earth.

Even a little pocketknife stuffed in his jeans gave a farm boy a sense of completeness. You could reach in and pull it out whenever someone asked if you had your pocketknife with you. It didn't matter that you couldn't open the blade by yourself. Just having one was proof that you were a practical farmer and stockman who was always prepared.

I didn't become a cotton baron. If I had, that first pocketknife would have been reason enough to haul every boll to Shep's gin. As things turned out, Shep had to settle for my paying out his coffee at Maurine's Green Frog Cafe now and again.

Pocketknives are openers of feed sacks, packaging and cans, cutters of baling twine, substitute screwdrivers.

They are the means to impromptu cantaloupe and watermelon feasts in the field, splitters of ripe apples and peaches, testers of the maturity of green cotton bolls in the fall.

A good pocketknife is a must when scratching around in the warming soil to find sprouting cotton, corn or maize a few days after planting. It becomes an instrument of decision when a shower has crusted the soil surface just as the young crop is struggling to emerge. A few pokes at the crusty soil with the pocketknife become the basis of putting a rotary hoe in the field.

Pocketknives have served as instruments of livestock surgery for as long as farming and ranching have gone on.

Electricians and phone crewmen and auto mechanics would be lost without their pocketknives. No electrical wiring would be stripped for connection, no interrupted telephone service restored.

Probably a lot of turnrow conversations over the years would not have become animated if not for the fact that the participants had their pocketknives.

Brief encounters at the edge of fields became neighborly visits once the parties climbed from their pickups, drew out their pocketknives and leaned against the fenders or sat on the running boards. The essential pocketknives came into play for cleaning nails, whittling sticks, cutting chaws from plugs, and scratching diagrams in the hard-packed surface of the turnrow.

With these spit-and-whittle, chew cane and visit times, folks get to know each other, and the country is closer.

The best of letter openers, bait cutters, fish gutters and bird cleaners, pocketknives are almost always in need of sharpening. Coaxing an edge from their blades with a stone is a skill unto itself that I wish I had mastered.

They are eminently practical, so much so that you hardly ever see one thrown away, though losing them is regrettably common. They have a way of leaping off of implement toolbars, pickup tailgates, tractor fenders, engine compartments, corral posts and barn braces after they have been put down for a moment. In certain shameful instances, they may even be "borrowed" and walk away. They hide in fresh-turned earth, weeds, grass, asphalt and concrete. Usually their getaway goes unnoticed until you next reach for them.

If you lost an Old Timer with one broken blade and another long, round-ended one over by the Umbarger railroad crossing a couple of years ago, rest assured that it is rehabilitated. I found it shining in the roadway and picked it up. The round blade, though worn, still works great for stripping wire and digging weeds out of my yard. I carry a smaller Buck for everyday uses like opening mail and packages.

Hopefully, somebody got some good out of a not-much-used Buck Stockman that got away from me down in the Hart country back when... I wasn't finished with it yet.

Trace Elements
Some occur naturally in the soil — and some are absorbed by country folk.

We have for years, in the farm country, been putting down nitrogen, potassium and phosphorus—N, P, and K—toward the end of producing the highest crop yields or the most forage possible per acre.

Sometimes, there is the need to add trace elements—rather obscure stuff like iron or zinc or manganese, that we don't think about every day. You've got to have sufficient amounts of this stuff to get the all-out production magic of healthy plants. Neglect it, and leaves turn anemically yellow, plants curl, and are stunted and unproductive.

N, P, K, and trace elements, applied as indicated by proper soil testing, promote desirable plant characteristics and activities. Nitrogen and iron give vigorous-growing plants with deep green foliage. Potassium and phosphorus help plants put on a good load of large fruit and retain that fruit until harvest with the help of a well-developed root system. Good roots feed the plant and anchor it to the soil.

A lot of the trace stuff can be found already present in the soil—sort of a natural gift that may have to be supplemented only in unusual circumstances.

The clays and sands and loams of the Plains soil are the stuff that a hardy people are rooted in, too. Plains soil contains the natural gift of other trace elements that aren't going to show up on any assay map.

There's a whole alphabet of these "gift traces"—As and Bs, Cs and Gs, Hs and Os.

We can't know how they came to be so much a part of things here. They must literally lie within the soil and somehow be taken up by our roots.

Affability, amicability, benevolence, compassion, congeniality, cordiality, generosity, helpfulness, humor, optimism, politeness—these nurturing "traces" lie beyond the sample bottles and the microscopic gaze of the soil chemist. Yet, if the harvest yields true, they must have been there, bestowing nourishment, filling the seed heads.

Pullman and Amarillo, Estacado, Friona and Randall and Olton, Bippus and Potter, Glenrio, Lincoln and Lofton and Lazbuddie, Pep and Portales and Redona clays and loams and sands hold these "traces" within. The "traces" lie beneath the carpeting of buffalo and sideoats, blue grama and

Western wheatgrass, vine mesquite, sand dropseed and Eastern gamagrass on the pasturelands.

You can tell who they are—these well-rooted people of the Plains. They have drawn the unseen traces to the surface and they pass them around—sharing nourishment for body, mind and soul.

The wise in ways of husbandry reseed and plow back the unassayable, priceless trace elements so that we will always have these essentials for living on the Plains.

The Sole Saver

With stitching, glue, leather, nails and neoprene, he gave worn foot-gear another chance.

A good pair of boots is like an old friend: comfortable, reliable, much appreciated. Life exerts wear and tear. Holes come with experience gained. You don't discard an old friend just because they get a little worn. The holes and broken stitches, thin soles and worn heel caps come with honorable service.

Back before he went into another line of work, when my Tony Lamas and Justins needed rehabilitation, I would go see my buddy John, over Canyon way. He worked out of a little shop with a boot painted on a plyboard sign that hung out front. The sign unpretentiously proclaimed John's service to the world.—He was a sole saver.

Before he sold the farm and took up other work, John was also an unreformed stock farmer. Because of this, he was into salvage, reclamation, rehabilitation and creation. He put these talents to good use in boot repair in hopes of supporting his bad habit of stock farming.

He used glue and stitching, nails, neoprene and leather and gave boots and shoes that had fallen on hard times another chance. Just as long as folks kept bringing them back and there was anything left of the foot-gear to patch, John would try.

He would repair sport shoes, handbags, boat tarps, volunteer fire department bunker gear, rope bags, real cowboy chaps and belts and a holster or two, and of course, boots and shoes—most anything with leather in its pedigree.

His shop was as functional as the ranch country. When I started calling there, the ribcage and skull of a cow were rigged upright on a frame in the window, a beat-up old Stetson cocked atop the skull. This *avant-garde* statuary might be entitled "Dry Fall: No Wheat Pasture," to accurately reflect the outlook of cows and cow people in these all-too-common circumstances on the Texas High Plains.

John's shop smelled of leather and glue. Bridles and chaps-in-progress, or awaiting a new owner in a swap, hung all about. Floor space was at a premium on account of a half-dozen saddles draped over barrels or sawhorses. Some of the saddles sported bright new leather where John had given them attention. A couple needed a new owner, having garnered previous experience "standing behind" cowboys riding wheat pasture and roping.

The cash register counter was papered with notices of hay and hogs and tack and horses and Blue Heeler and Rottweiler puppies for sale. Being a stockman, John would often broker a little red top cane or haygrazer hay between farmers who had extra, and stockmen with hungry cows to feed who sure needed some. This end of the business was especially notable in those rare times when a decent snow fell on the wheat country.

At the east side of his shop, John had sort of a "back door" room where he did tack work. Hanging on the door was a big moth-eaten bearskin rug that some fellow gave him. John told kids who came into his shop that he wrestled that bear for his coat and won two out of three falls. John has never been one to unduly embellish a story.

You had to wade around the corner of the cash register counter to get to the south room. That is where the serious business was carried on. John's work area was crammed with shelves cluttered with footwear that had fallen from the straight and narrow. Each pair of foot-gear was tagged with names and particulars, and promises of when reformations would be completed.

One corner held wooden stand-ins for feet, used in custom hand-making of boots. Boxes of sole and heel pad material, big sewing machines, lathe-like machinery for shaping and polishing leather, small anvils for hammer work, were found here.

The west wall's calendar advertised the wares of a wholesale leather distributor in San Angelo. A western print on another wall depicted a Longhorn cow with fire in her eyes. She stood over her calf, warily watching a coyote that had seriously underestimated the price of veal—a message appreciated by the proprietor, who, against all economic good sense, ran a few calves on wheat.

John, in cap and glue-spattered, black-stained apron, worked in one corner of this room where he draped boots and shoes over a metal stand for the hammering. This work area was close enough to the stove and the sliding metal door at the back that he could absorb warmth in the winter and catch cooling breezes in the summer. He wielded hammer and brush and cutting tools in this corner, shaping repairs, glopping on glue liberally, not worrying about how much got on his apron. He moved swiftly to snap brads in place or punch holes in belting. When he ran up stitching on a machine, the pace was slow and steady. He had broken enough dollar-apiece needles to know it was a lot less needle-costly that way.

John held court with cowboys and farmers, cooks, professors and students from West Texas A&M University, just down the road, lawyers and housewives, even people of the cloth. Most anybody who wanted their boots or their shoes or their purse fixed dropped in.

You might say that John sort-of traded even with the clergy. John could fix shoes for a *padre* or a preacher and honestly say, with a knowing smirk, that he had saved their sole.

One time as I arrived, John was finishing a custom pair of amazingly soft white glove-leather chaps. Sensibly, he had waited to size the belt so that he wouldn't have to cut off any brad work. The proud owner was trying the chaps on for size. John guesstimated the belt length correctly. All he had to do was punch a few holes in the belt so that it could be buckled, clamp a couple of brads in place, and one Happy cowboy was set to ride.

John would fix my boots while I waited—unheard-of today at almost any other boot shop. The heel pads on mine were often worn so thin that my knees ached. He'd tell me to kick them off.

I'd perch, sock-footed, on a shop-made stool and try to make myself useful. Once, I ran leather laces through a pair of chaps that had years of experience rubbing against saddle leather. John showed me how to do the lacing. I weaved the rawhide strips and thought that this must be the Texas lacing leather that I have always heard about being tougher than.

To the whumping of the cobbler's hammer against new neoprene pads, John and I talked about wheat pasture, doctoring calves, feeding show hogs high-dollar feed, what it would be like to win a pile of cash in the lottery. If he won, a fellow could just farm and pasture stock until he ran through every last dime. Wouldn't take long, but it would sure be fun making the run and getting the experience.

Ever-practical John explained the way that a small stock farmer ought to look at the hog business—hogs, in John's opinion, having the considerable advantage of never making their owner more than ten dollars a head, and never losing more than a hundred.

I learned that John was not just a formidable livestock baron. He had a really great deal going with his boot shop. He bought half-soles for ten bucks, turned around and sold them for five, put them on worn-out boots for free and customers flocked in... John said it sure beat the heck out of farming—irrigated or dryland—or pasturing cattle on dried-out wheat.

Finishing his nailing and trimming work, John would flick on a machine, shape the heels on my black boots, shine them a bit on a rotating brush and hand them back to me.

Renewed cushioning beneath the heels invariably made me feel two inches taller. The familiar Tony Lamas, comfortable once more, were good for a few more miles.

John had worked a minor miracle and saved them again.

I sometimes played havoc with his "great business deal" math and slapped a twenty on the counter.

Seemed little enough to pay for a sole's salvation.

Working Logic

Only on Wall Street would people having jobs be seen as a bad thing.

Wall Street never makes sense... It is a panic-driven "Chicken Little," yet it leads the country around by the nose.

The stock market crash in the vanguard of the Dirty 30's once led a trip-to-hell-in-a-handcart for the economy. There was, then, correlation between events on Wall Street and what was happening to the man on the street, or the back 40 acres... People suddenly had no jobs and that meant no income to spend on goods and services. With far too many people having no means of supporting themselves and their families, there was a lot of doing-without. The country required a long time to pull itself up by the bootstraps and might not have accomplished it nearly so quickly had it not been for the impetus provided, tragically, by the requisite mobilization for a war effort.

Today, the stock market can fall out of bed by over a hundred points in one day, due to a higher-than-expected rate of employment.

There is about as much sound logic in the way that the market reacts to this sort of news as there is in the way that 99 sheep will follow one errant wooly that bolts through the fence onto some coyote's all-you-can-eat mutton buffet tray, or the way that a flock of domestic turkeys, hearing thunder, pile bird-upon-bird in the corner of the poultry yard and smother.

What gives here? The market panics because more people are working. That is bad news?

Maybe Wall Street seldom makes sense because it doesn't have any.

The nation's genuine wealth—not the speculated-at-on-paper kind—springs from countryside, heartland and daily honest effort by working folk to give a fair day's work for their pay. It comes of striving to build community, common purpose and respect.

Real riches stem from the energy in sunshine, soil and nurturing rainwater transformed into diverse plant and animal life. These captured energy forms, in turn, pass on their own, be it protein, or proactive involvement, up the chain, to sustain other life. Even at the top of the chain, energy is passed along to continue the cycle. This is not anything to touch off a panic.

Much is realized from real work. It nets sore muscles, calloused hands, tired backs, work ethic, wheat and corn and sorghum and beans in the bin, cotton packed tightly in the bale, beef and pork and lamb and goat on-the-hoof, sturdy stands of grass and ponds of stock water in the pastures, coveys of quail, pheasants, fleet deer, elusive turkey, great flights of ducks and geese and cranes, decent kids, good neighbors, strong relationships upon and over the land, all fruits of dedicated labor and care.

The worth of work need not be measured solely by what is hauled across the scales at the elevator or gin or feedyard, or yielded in stock dividends and compounding interest.

Satisfaction, sense of self and community, good health, friendship, accomplishment, appreciation of nature, self-respect, even pure old unadulterated happiness, are work dividends.

Labor with the Lord, the elements, four and two-legged critters, head and hands, heart and health for long enough, and if there is any sense at all hidden between the ears there in that melon holding up your *sombrero*, you ought to know and understand that work, done honorably and well, whether at minimum wage, high dollar, or volunteered without wage, has worth that cannot be measured by the standards of a marketplace maelstrom.

As my wife, Kerrie, is fond of saying: *"The people who do the most important work don't get paid for it."*

Rhyme by the Road

Burma-Shave signs along the roadways once provided clever endearing prose. Here's a stab at a few for today.

Burma-Shave advertising signs were a cherished feature along rural American roadsides. Pithy verses painted on small signposts that were erected at carefully-spaced intervals gave folks a chuckle and delivered an effective advertising message for shaving cream at the same time. Just for grins, let's try a few.

Warning notice to be displayed above a rural telephone cooperative's underground lines:

> HAVE A CARE
> DON'T LEAVE US HARRIED
> THIS IS WHERE
> OUR CABLE'S BURIED

How about this comment on a phone cooperative's modernization?

> OUR PHONES DELIVER
> SERVICE FINE
> SINCE WE GOT RID
> OF PARTY LINES

Here's one to post on 18-wheelers hauling feedlot cattle:

> THIS BIG RIG
> IS RUNNING FULL
> PLEASE STAY BACK
> WE COULD SLING BULL

A roadside teaser for the Dawn Cafe...

>COME ON IN
>FOR GOOD EATIN'
>WANDA BURGERS
>CAN'T BE BEATEN

Here's a fickle weather truism to display along the curving road at Fellers Farms:

>WE GROW HAY
>AND WE GROW GRAIN
>WE'D GROW MORE
>IF IT WOULD RAIN!

On the welcome mat at the offices of Texas Panhandle feedyards:

>WE FEED CATTLE
>AS YOU CAN TELL
>COME ON IN
>DON'T MIND THE SMELL

In pheasant hunting country:

>IF YOU BELIEVE
>PHEASANTS ARE KEEN
>PLEASE DON'T LEAVE
>YOUR FIELDS TOO CLEAN

On the road to Andrews Produce:

>WE'VE GOT BLACKEYES
>WE'VE GOT SQUASH
>WE EVEN RAISE
>SOME CAIN, BYGOSH

On the outskirts of a dust-fogged feedlot town:

> AROUND THESE PARTS
> OUR AIR'S NOT THIN
> WE CAN SEE
> WHAT WE BREATHE IN

Posted by parents with kids attending universities:

> HERE AND NOW
> WE DO ACKNOWLEDGE
> ALL OUR MONEY'S
> GONE TO COLLEGE

Along the road down San Angelo way, in sheep country:

> RAISING SHEEP
> IS NO PARTY
> 'CAUSE THE COYOTES
> SURE EAT HEARTY!

Posted in front of a community church that's not picky:

> WE TAKE SINNERS
> BACKSLIDERS, TOO
> WE'LL EVEN TAKE
> THE LIKES OF YOU!

The G-Man

Credentials can be downright impressive.

Farmers and ranchers like to keep an eye on who's coming and going around the place. Things can sprout legs and walk off.

A local fellow told me a while back about a strange vehicle that drove onto his property last summer. The driver got out, entered his pasture and started looking around. The farmer wasn't sure what the fellow was looking for.

Concerned that this stranger might not know about the potentially troublesome flora and fauna hereabouts, and thinking that he might even be able to help the guy, the local farmer drove over to the pasture. He climbed out of his rattletrap pickup, howdied the stranger and asked what he was doing in the pasture.

"It's okay, I'm with the government," the stranger proclaimed with utter confidence, whipping a card from his shirt pocket.

The card was right colorful and identified the fellow as an employee of one of those government agencies. There were lightning bolts, some kind of bird's tailfeathers and weird-looking weeds on the logo etched in the card.

"Might wanna' be real careful which pasture you get into out here," the farmer advised, friendly-like.

"Sir, I am extensively trained to perform the job that I have been sent here by my agency to do. I have been given full authorization to go where I want, when I want, and to do whatever I feel is necessary. I can handle whatever situation arises. I do not require your permission to be here. I would prefer that you cooperate by not interfering with my work," the suit-type shot back, tersely.

"But I was just gonna..."

"Sir! I cannot proceed with my assessment of this property's compliance with Section 8, subparagraph 22 of Regulation D, pertaining to codus XXXX, slash seven, as amended, of the decree protecting the square-roller tumblebug if you persist in bothering me!"

The G-man was turning red in the face and starting to squirm like he was standing in a red ant bed, though as far as the farmer could tell, dadburn, he wasn't.

He could see that he was going to get nowhere with this guy, so the farmer climbed back into his pickup and drove off. Since age had rendered the old pickup sorta' rumbly and creaky, the G-man apparently didn't hear his mumbling about just seeing whose—what did he call it—ass-essment—held shucks.

The farmer didn't get to finish tightening the loose span in the fence that he had gone back to work on. He heard a desperate-sounding cry.

Looking up from throwing some wire wraps around a fence post, he saw that the G-man was hot-hoofing-it across the pasture.

The bull that the farmer had tried to warn the G-man about was fixin' to snort calf slobbers in that dressy dude's hip pocket.

"Help! Save me," the G-man yelped.

Though he had tried to prevent it, now that the rodeo was underway, the farmer could think of only one thing he could do that would be of much help.

He cupped his hands around his mouth, megaphone-style, so his voice would carry, and hollered words of sage advice:

"Show 'im your card!"

Things Work Out

Life's events have a way of resolving themselves.

Things work out...

In hardscrabble times when an old hen had to suffer outlandish pain to lay a dollar's worth of eggs, folks got by with what they had. Most everybody had a few cows to milk, even if they were so wild that it took everybody on the place and two neighbors to hold bossy down.

Often, there was way more milk than even a large family could drink so the hogs' diet included skim milk. A fair amount of butter was churned, and milk was clabbered for cottage cheese.

Some folks "buttered up" the wagon. Leaving the salt out and adding a little tar for coloring yielded dairy-based axle grease. There was no money for the petroleum-based product. Greasing at home and greasing again in Tulia generally got you there and back. If there was some doubt, you unhitched about midway and greased again.

Things work out...

In times past, three fellows were going cross-country in an old Model T Ford. They were a number of miles from home, crossing a pasture, when a tire went flat.

They broke the tire down on the spot to fix it, and discovered that they were going to need a lining flap if they didn't want to make a long walk home.

What could they use for the lining flap? One of the fellows who lived a little higher-on-the-hog than the others was wearing a new pair of silk drawers—but not for long. By majority rule those silk drawers were forfeited for the cause and cut up to serve the purpose. The three fellows rode home courtesy of a very stylish lining flap.

Things work out...

A stock broker friend, Ike Stevens, has offered sage advice many times: "Sometimes the bulls win, sometimes the bears win, but a pig never wins."

Some folks who owned a fine young stud horse back-when could probably appreciate that remark.

This slick stud horse caught the eye of many a passerby. A promising hunk of horseflesh just coming into prime, the stud had not proved a full-fledged working horse yet since he had not made the trip to Tulia-and-back in working harness.

Still, the horse was impressive enough. Several folks made offers to buy him.

One serious buyer just had to have that hoss. Wanted him so badly that he finally offered $10 far-and-away above what the stud horse was worth.

The folks who owned the stud horse thought the offer over. If that stud was worth all that much, maybe they had better keep him.

The prize stud was penned with the other draft horses and mules that night.

One of the resident mules had figured out how to get grain whenever he wanted it, and was smart enough to limit how much he ate.

The mule would slip open the gate latch, back up to the granary door and deliver a few well-aimed kicks. The jarring caused grain to spill around the granary door onto the ground where old long-ears could get at it.

Maybe the wooden granary door was getting rotten. Maybe the mule was showing off to the stud horse and kicked extra hard—the granary door broke and unleashed an avalanche of grain.

The stud came out of the corral, poked his head in the pile of grain, and ate like a horse.

Next morning, the owners discovered that their slick stud horse that had brought a buyer's bid $10 over his worth had filled his gut with grain, foundered, and expired.

No matter how smart you think you are in a deal, some jasshonkey will come along and show you up.

Things work out...

Tommy, a local cowman, has a fine blue heeler, Boo. He takes Boo with him everywhere.

That Boo is a mighty smart dog. He stays right alongside the boss, does whatever Tommy tells him, and balances masterfully on top of Tommy's pickup toolbox, even during sharp turns.

Tommy was figuring on wintering some cows. Like cowmen have to do, he went with his hat in his hands to call on Wedge, the banker. Tommy was hoping to set up a line of credit for feed against a spring calf crop.

Being a fine dog, Boo went into the bank with Tommy. Boo padded into Wedge's office, sniffed around a little, thought about hiking a leg at the corner of the banker's desk, but had manners-enough not to, circled four times, and laid down at Tommy's side to offer moral support.

Wedge didn't see any way that the bank could extend Tommy a

loan—and in characteristic fashion, was pretty blunt in saying so. By way of punctuation, he loudly proclaimed that he didn't want any mangy mutt in his office, either!

Tommy was disappointed in Wedge's answer—though given the cattle market, it was about what he had expected. They didn't call that banker Wedge for nothing!

Finances had nothing to do with a dog's pedigree though. Somehow, the cow dog sensed the slander.

Boo moved in a righteous blur. Wedge frog-hopped atop his desk with Boo snarling at his heels. The dog snatched a cuff and Wedge was quickly wearing short britches on one leg.

Boo, shaking his head, spat out pieces of dress slack fabric, bolted from the banker's office and nipped at three other people on the way out of the bank.

"What's gotten into that dog of yours? He sure seems browned-off." Pat, another cowman, quizzed in amazement as he met Boo and Tommy beating a hasty exit from the bank.

Pat watched Tommy open the tailgate of his pickup. Boo jumped in and perched in his customary place atop the cross-bed toolbox, still shaking his head and making smacking sounds with his lolling tongue.

Tommy closed the tailgate, turned and looked Pat square in the eye.

"Ain't a thing wrong with my dog. Boo was just tryin' ta get the banker taste outta' his mouth!"

Elevator View

Maybe we should all look at our world from the top of a grain elevator...just to gain proper perspective.

Looking at the world from the top of a country elevator can lend perspective. I can remember going up in a lift with my uncle at one of the local elevators at Hart once, but at that time all of the steel and concrete made for keenly-felt uncertainty about riding up or down in a little metal cage that didn't look at all reassuring.

A lot of years passed between that first tour and the next one. Lonnie McFarland, the manager of the former Sherley-Anderson elevator over at Lariat, now the AGP Grain Cooperative, "the world's largest country elevator" based on the size and number of its concrete grain storage tanks, gave me a dime tour of his facility a few years ago.

Lonnie wanted to help me get the best pictures for a story and figured that going "up top" of the concrete storage tanks would afford an excellent photo opportunity.

Lonnie piled me onto a man lift and hauled me to the top of a section of the concrete storage bins that are over 100 feet tall, explaining the mechanical workings of grain elevators as we went.

I was nodding, letting-on that I was taking it all in, and possibly even absorbing some of it, but standing at the back of the lift cage leaving fingernail marks in its expanded metal sides with one hand, clutching my camera with the other, and hoping the electricity didn't suddenly play out and strand this heights-shy guy somewhere in the bowels of this great concrete colossus.

While an emergency ladder was within easy reach at any time, as I watched the rungs passing the front of the lift during the long ride up, its presence was pretty slim comfort. The idea of having to climb down a ladder while trying to keep a camera from beating me to death, breaking a lens, or missing a rung had no appeal at all.

Lonnie put me completely at ease. He said there had been a power failure a few days before...One of his workmen had to climb down the ladder. Happened all of the time...How reassuring. Wonder if he suspected that his lift cage passenger was the type who isn't even wild about climbing to the top of a stepladder?

We reached the "Texas House" and solid footing. Given the ride up, stepping out on top of one of the guard-railed bins wasn't too bad.

The world was vastly different looking from this vantage point than at ground level. The countryside became a great patchwork quilt—brown and green and ocher squares and circles, broken by seams that were roads and railways.

Verdant farmlands all around us were the familiar pieces of this coverlet. Symmetrical circles amidst blocky fields gave evidence of the sprinkler pivots where the silvery aluminum machines, made by man, poured out trickles of life-giving water to the crops in their pre-programmed rounds. Though tall-looking from the ground, the sprinkler towers were like tinker toys from up here. Their water delivery was puny against the amount of rain that could fall from the skies when the clouds finally opened.

Rows of corn and sorghum and beans and sugar beets were well-defined. The farmlands were stitched together into a whole that blanketed the earth as far as the eye could see. This intricate pattern was not the work of human hands alone.

From up here the world seemed a lot smaller and more closely linked. Muleshoe and Lazbuddie, Farwell and Friona and Bovina, Summerfield and Hereford, all distant neighbors when traveling the highway down there and our long view of things is obscured by corn and sorghum patches, were all neighbors close at hand now. Each was just down the narrow bands of road from the other, sprouting from the same good earth as the crops.

In each of those other places there were concrete structures like the one on which we were standing. These were great storehouses where the fruits of labor in this heartland could be gathered.

Maybe these were also watchtowers for folks in each of these places to climb from time to time to gain perspective: Lofty places to ponder our seeding in close rows down there, where the quilt sustains us.

You may feel like a pretty big wheel down there, but from up here, it's easy to see that against the layout of green and amber and brown patchwork stretching from one horizon to another, we are all just individual stitches in the humbling quilt of life.

Communion

We can share something sacred not just in church, but on a turnrow, in a wheat field, on a trout stream, in the kitchen, in the company of pheasant hunters.

Com-mun-ion: 1. Act of sharing; community of condition or relation; participation 2. A body of Christians having one common faith and discipline, as the Anglican *Communion* 3. The sacrament of the Eucharist; also, the service (**communion service**, or, in Anglican churches, **Holy Communion**) or the part of the Mass in which the consecrated elements are partaken of

    We wonder over a ceremonial sharing of bread—a food common to us all—in a ritual that can be all-inclusive—yet sadly, can be rendered highly exclusive for reasons of doctrine.

    In some churches the congregation and guests say prayers, reminders, remembrances, and an invitation is issued to all to share in an "open" ceremony. The faithful partake of morsels of square or round cracker, or bits of bread, and sip grape juice from little thumb-and-forefinger-fitting plastic cups. What they share in reverence is communion.

    Amidst another denomination just down the street, a priest consecrates bread and wine to the rhythmic wrist-English of an altar boy who jangles bells as a reminder to the faithful to pay attention and be mindful and reverent toward something important happening in their midst. Subsequently, only those of the denomination may come forward to partake of sacramental bread and wine—body and blood—Communion.

    Not all of us share communion at the hands of a priest, a preacher, an elder or deacon, or a lay leader.

    A good many summers ago, my Dad and I stopped the pickup at the irrigation well on the north end of my aunt's farm. Dad tinkered with a few settings, checked the engine oil level, went to the gearhead and adjusted the flow of the drip tube slightly, so that lubricant would flow down the pump column. He hooked the cables to a fresh, hot battery, then jockeying with fingers of both hands, simultaneously depressed the oil pressure button and the ignition switch, while working the choke lever.

The starter whined and the green-painted Chrysler industrial engine growled and thumped as it turned over, then coughed to life with a puff of exhaust smoke.

Dad expertly shoved in the choke and adjusted the throttle to a fast idle, holding down the Murphy switch bypass until the oil pressure built up.

Once the pressure gauge confirmed that oil was coursing through the engine, he opened the throttle to rev the engine, then slowly pushed in the clutch lever to engage the driveshaft linked to the gearhead.

As the driveshaft began to turn, the engine lugged with the load. Dad worked the throttle to gradually pour on the coal. The engine thrummed and the gearhead whined up to working speed.

After a short interval accentuated by the thunder of the Chrysler, underground rain gushed from the pump's discharge pipe and splashed over the cooling coils in the bottom of the concrete engine platform, tumbling out the spillway, roiling about, pooling and building volume before coursing down the newly-cut ditch that transected the end of the maize field.

After the well ran a bit and the sand cleared from the flow stream, Dad went to the pickup, grabbed a bucket, caught it full of water from the discharge pipe, then climbed up the front of the engine platform. He opened the radiator cap, poured in this natural coolant, and screwed the cap back down. He walked around the engine, checking the oil sight gauge, the pressure, the sweet sound of smooth running. Once he was satisfied that the engine was right, we climbed into the pickup and rattled southward down the west turnrow, quickly passing the leaf and debris-foamed column of water rolling along in the ditch.

At the south end of the ditch run Dad let the pickup coast to a stop. We bailed out and he grabbed a shovel and a span of canvas and began setting a ditch stop while I grabbed armfuls of two-inch siphon tubes from the back of the pickup and scattered them where we would make the first set.

The curved aluminum tubes clunked hollowly in place, half in the ditch, half in the furrows between the rows of thirsty grain sorghum.

Once we had worked up a sweat scattering the tubes and setting the ditch stops, there was nothing to do but wait for the water to travel the length of the ditch to reach us.

We plopped down on the running board, on the shady side of the pickup. Resting in this makeshift place of comfort, we could hear the distant drone of the hard-working Chrysler in its striving to bring life-giving Ogallala water to the surface. Other far-off wells on neighboring farms joined in the chorus that was intermittently heard, then silent, depending on the air currents.

There was something comforting to a farm boy in the constant, faraway sounds of droning Chevy and Ford and Chrysler irrigation engines, the throaty purr of big Molines—a sound missed when they fell silent.

In the cool shade of the pickup, sitting there and keeping our rubber irrigation booted-feet out of the hot sun, we were serenaded by the rustle of the twisted, pineapple-like leaves of the parched sorghum as breeze touched them. This was a pleasant moment of keeping the faith, waiting for the water that would slake the thirst of the maize. We talked of crops and their care, things of life and its living, shared fellowship on the running board.

On the west turnrow at the end of a maize field in the middle of July, our wine was water drawn earlier at the well, and guzzled from a dripping canvas bag that kept it cool. This was one of many times, in the midst of daily farm work, that we shared communion.

On the South Fork of the Rio Grande, in a little Colorado canyon hidden by towering blue spruce, I found a place of water calm enough to wade, with promising pools for fly-fishing.

Water-worn boulders angled into a stand of spruce on one bank. In the eddies adjacent the boulders and a clot of spruce roots that reached into the eroded edge of the riverbank were wonderful trout-harboring pools and slicks.

Wading cautiously, pausing every few steps to watch, I eased toward the big boulder pool. A trout rose and noisily slashed a caddis floating atop a backswirl.

Wind was flowing down the canyon, into my face, bringing challenge with the smell of streamside foliage. The requisite upstream casting would be difficult.

Working the light four-weight rod, I paid out line, attempting to lay down a dry fly on the water next to the boulder. Wind eddies foiled one cast after another.

The challenge was to quietly wade close, wait on the wind—time a cast between puffs and shoot the line forward. This was a work of rhythm so intense I forgot about the fish.

My world was a push-pull motion, a close watch on the bluish-green floating line and the length of leader and tippet when they shot forward at the urging of the fly rod.

In an instant of abandoning all but what was in front of me, I sensed only the flowing of the stream, the soughing of fly line through the rod guides, the rustle of spruce limbs, the ripple of water.

A beaver surfaced midstream to swim in circles and eye me cautiously.

Upstream, a mule deer tiptoed to the edge of the water, then turned nervously to stare at me. She froze in a long glance, then went back to her drink. My casting didn't alarm her.

Overhead, a pair of eagles screamed and climbed in a towering circle toward their nearby mountain cliff dwelling.

I was working the fly to a symphony of sounds and sensations. The Adams I was casting bumped against the boulder and dropped into the slick water.

The fly floated perfectly for only a heartbeat. A slashing strike brought the line taut as I raised my rod.

The sensation of an electrical shock pulsed through the fly rod and into my arm.

A sleek rainbow trout spattered spray with its tail as it leaped from the pool, springing as high as the tops of the boulders before falling back.

The fish rushed hard into the current where the stream boiled around the boulders and raced into the main channel.

Clumsily I turned to go with the fish, stumbling frantically in the streambed rocks and gravel, nearly falling as the reel screamed and gave line.

Fragile tippet withstood power surges of strain. The rod tip pumped hard as the good fish raced amidst a large, flat pool. *Patience, don't rush this and break the leader*. The hard tugs eased. I gained line, a few feet at a time. Working the fish into the quiet edge of a shallow pool, I dropped to a knee where the water spilled over a gravel bar, easing the trout to the surface and within reach by lifting the rod high with my right hand, gently touching the fish with my left. With a wiggle of thumb and forefinger I released the dry fly's hook. The rainbow-hued fish powered away.

I lingered there, at once spent and thrilled. Perhaps it was a genuflection, dropping to my knee in the shallow water that rolled over the sand and gravel. I was in a sacred place. The cathedral spires were mountains and towering blue spruce that eagles soared above. Wild creatures, soft breezes, tumbling water and rustling limbs were celebrants offering up prayers of praise to their Maker.

I took communion with them.

Wheat harvest—incredible in its abundance—was in full swing in the late days of June. A winter snow had gifted the dryland farms of western Deaf Smith County with the moisture that can sometimes turn the countryside to wheat—and it had—stands were yielding a fantastic 80 bushels an acre.

Invited to photograph the spectacle of such rare plenty, I traveled to a sprawling expanse of dryland wheat fields where a convoy of four big green John Deere combines and grain hauling equipment were working.

Wives brought supper to the field in the back of Suburbans. In the shade of trucks, grain carts and combines, a table was spread on tailgates—a sharing of bread in the midst of the gathering of the staff of life.

The pause for food was peaceful but brief, the drivers mounted their machines once more, the combines belched diesel smoke and clouds of dust and chaff and rolled again.

Camera strapped around my neck, I roamed a vast field of amber wheat rippling in the wind.

Through the lens I saw anew the glow of sun against western clouds, the choreography of machines gathering a gift, the richness of the land poured in great golden streams into the beds of waiting trucks. The inner workings of my camera used light to paint a picture on film.

Wall Street will never own-up to it, but the real wealth of this nation is displayed in vast fields where families keep the humming combines threshing grain, augering mounds of hard red winter wheat into trucks that lumber down country roads and highways to the elevators that are storage vaults for the wealth of the land.

Crouched there in the midst of an amber ocean of grain, I watched swaying expanses of ripe wheat form rolling waves. Through the viewfinder I composed scenes of closely-focused individual bearded heads against broad skies. I snapped still more meek attempts to capture a fleeting image of the transformation of sunlight energy to grain. Seed and soil, moisture, man's feeble cultivation and God's beneficence come together in golden grains of communion.

The late Raymond and Emma Smith used to spoil legions of goose and pheasant hunters. They extended the most gracious hospitality at their home near Ford, in northern Deaf Smith County. They lived on the southeast shore of what was once one of the finest goose lakes in all of the Texas Panhandle—and not a bad pheasant cover, either.

Emma was a first-rate cook, and particularly shined in that capacity during the opening weekend of pheasant season each year, assisted by her daughter, Katy, and daughter-in-law, Maudette. The Smith ladies displayed not only graciousness, but great tolerance for tracked-in mud.

A fraternity of pheasant fanatics used to gather at the Smith farm for opening weekend. Among the "sports" at one time or another were Dr. Trow Mims and his son, Ed, local dentist "Hap" Cavness, Dr. Bill Lawrence and Dr. Irl Sell, "Little" Charlie Seeds, Tom Sieling and Charlie Broad from Dallas, Earl and Jerry Stultz, Mike and Paul and Toby Smith, and sometimes, even Raymond and Emma's son, John A, packing his old humpback Browning.

I was fortunate, being invited to join this cast of characters.

We enjoyed some years when the hunting was phenomenal, other years when bird numbers were thin and the hunters grew footsore and frustrated.

However the hunting went, there was always opening-day dinner at Emma's house to look forward to.

We would come dragging in about dinner-thirty—all aching muscles, exhaustion, and starvation. Bundled-up men dwindled before the eyes, peeling out of layers of insulated coveralls and jackets and game vests. Most of us lost at least 10 pounds just shedding mud-caked boots.

The fraternity was ushered into the feast with backslaps and handshakes and an enthusiastic come-in-this-house-you're welcome.

We told embellished stories of how the morning's hunting had gone until Emma hushed the hubbub for the turning of grace. Then she would shoo us into the kitchen to make the big pass around the grand buffet table that fairly sagged under the fruit of all of the efforts of the ladies who labored at the stove and the oven on behalf of their guests.

Turkey and ham and roast beef and multiple kinds of spuds, vegetables, and assorted salads and trimmings were set before us, along with homemade bread, and of course, Emma's pies and cobblers...all wonderful...all anybody could have ever wanted.

After Emma's huge feed, you needed a nap a lot worse than you needed to go back into the field to finish the limit.

Emma tended not just to us pheasant hunters with her kitchen talents, but to her neighbors and community at large. She helped with fund-raising dinners to benefit scholarship efforts. She "neighbored" with local ranchers Colby and Jim Conkwright in bringing food to their big annual registered Hereford cattle sale between Milo Center and Farmer's Corner.

Without fanfare or notoriety, Emma made her kitchen a ministry.

For 30 years she prepared communion bread for Sunday services at the old First Christian Church of Hereford. She did it weekly—for three decades—baking unleavened bread with no yeast or salt.

To Emma, it was no trouble at all. After her passing, the family found the communion bread recipe still there, taped to the inside of a cabinet door in her kitchen.

Fittingly, unleavened communion bread got made for all of those years by a woman who was the salt of the earth.

The sacrament of communion involves the breaking of bread and the sharing of fellowship.

A gathering of cattle buyers, or a harvest crew, the assembling of a fraternity of hunters, quiet moments on the running board of a pickup parked on a turnrow, inspiring instants wading in a trout stream or crouched in a stand of wheat undulating like sea waves to the horizon may not seem particularly religious.

I cherish such gatherings and moments, in the same way that I cherish rare instances of unity when denominations share faith held in common rather than nutpick over their differences.

All give hope, a sense of oneness, and feed body and soul.

Such times are sacred.

Hoe Hands

We sold our sweat cheap, battling pigweed, kochia and Johnsongrass and learning work-brittleness.

Basic inputs were cheap—a hoe, a file to keep it sharp, a can of insect repellent, a cap, possibly a pair of gloves, and a jug or jar or bag of water.

The sweat part of occupying much of your summer battling weeds in crops was "cheap" only relative to how you felt about spending your time swinging the hoe.

Time was the commodity that farm kids had the most of in the summer. Some didn't mind trading a lot of theirs—and physical labor and blisters on their hands—for some spending money.

Hoeing can't be glamorized. It is a grueling means of making pocket money, but for a lot of youngsters it beat the heck out of no job. Even $1 an hour added up to some money eventually—if you spent enough hours out there swinging the two-handed cultivator.

We had our own hoe crew in our country. The Barham kids, David and Diane and Brenda, and sometimes, Ronnie, all neighbors from a couple of miles across the way, would work with my brother, Patrick, and me. Cousin Andy was around during one of the summers and worked with us, too.

We took turns meeting in our family yards on alternating mornings, just as the sun was rising. The air was still cool and pleasant at that hour, and dew hung heavy on the leaves. Files grated across the hoe blades, metallic rubbing of the ridges of the bastard and rat-tailed files shearing thin slivers of metal, imparting a keen edge to our tools.

A sharp hoe means easier cutting. Hoe very much and you are going to have a good file close at hand and use it often during a day. In some of the fields filled with Johnsongrass, monstrous red careless and tough kochia, a fine-edged, double-bitted axe would not have been out of order for whacking through the arm-sized trunks of pigweed towering within the cotton and corn and maize.

When it was time to go to the field, everyone piled in the old pickup, half of the workers sitting on the tailgate with legs dangling over the edge. The dog hopped aboard too, an ex-officio member of the crew.

We drove easy. No hurry to get to the field, no need to spill everybody out of the back.

Wasn't too bad as you started early in the morning. The day was cool and new enough that you could make a couple of throughs before the process got to be like work.

The sun came blazing up. By mid-morning, its heat bore down. The chuff, chuff, chuff of the hoe blades biting into the earth beneath weed roots was soon monotonous. With two hours to go until dinner, the brunt of the day was still ahead.

After-dinner tested staying power. With the sun bearing down fiercely and hardly a breeze stirring, this was a breathless time of the air hanging motionless, the sweat flowing freely and salty drops trickling into stinging eyes. Trips to the water jug came often.

Someone might bring a transistor radio, hung from their belt, and the sounds of top 40 music helped to pass the dragging hours of arm labor and burning feet as we shuffled through the hot soil, waging war on the weeds that were our collective nemesis and, ironically, our benefactor.

Blisters and mosquito bites and tired backs came with the territory. Our progress wasn't hard to track. The rows that we had walked looked like cleared forest compared to the remainder of the field.

The weeds were sometimes so tough and stubborn that a hoe handle would snap in the effort to grub their thieving roots free of the soil. The metal sometimes snapped in the crook at the neck of the hoe. Replacing a damaged hoe cost more than a hoe hand would make in a day. At times, we used a shovel to goose beneath the weeds and slice them off at the roots, making this tool work better than a hoe without as much risk of breaking.

If the crew could stand to work that late, the coolness that greeted us in the morning would gradually return with the evening air. Eight or ten hours of broiling in the sun was just about enough for even the most determined hoe hand.

Most folks who hired hoe hands paid promptly and regular, Friday afternoon, sometimes on Saturday. The hours had piled up steadily, and by the time a field was clean, the crew had some serious money coming—serious for kids our age, anyway.

One time we hoed a good part of a very nasty cotton patch, full of rank Johnsongrass, kochia, pigweed and blueweed rife with the proverbial tough rows to hoe. Our crew battled a jungle for nearly two weeks.

Finally, we had to stalk the landowner to get paid. When everybody collected and went to the bank, the checks bounced. Several in the crew were about ready to break a hoe handle after that deal—although it wouldn't have been on a stand of thick-trunked pigweed.

The hoe crew got tanned and toughened by the weather, the work, and sometimes, rotten economic reality. Even in farm country, not everybody is honest.

Hoe hands learned the work ethic and they got paid for it—most of the time.

Country kids who made their hands raw against a hoe handle in Johnsongrass patches learned their first lessons about work-brittleness—A dollar goes farther when its worth is measured against the blister scale.

Tractor Music

Some of the old ones may have sounded sweeter because they were so hard to start.

Something uniquely reassuring can be heard in the powerful, steady thrum, the purr, the pop, the roar, the rumble of a tractor engine. It is the sound of work getting done, deliverance from mudholes, soft ditches, wet turnrows.

Modern, noise-reducing cabs with their radios, tape decks, air conditioning and other conveniences are mighty nice, and for the cost of a rig these days, they ought to be. There is great relief in getting off of the tractor at the end of the day without your ears ringing and being able to hear normal-tone conversation after plowing.

The workhorses of the farm have become so technologically developed that they all sound alike. In bygone years, tractors had a sound that reflected their manufacturer and their personality.

From the time that tractors came to replace the raw muscle power of mules, one of the most cheerful summertime sounds on a farm was the rhythmic pop-pop-pop-pop of the old two-cylinders. This art form reached its peak with the dual-cylinder John Deeres that came to be affectionately known as "Popping Johnnies."

The popping of these tractors was evidence that someone was steadily plugging away at a farming chore, and making good progress at it. Poppers like the old Model A and subsequent models down the line persisted in fields from the early days into the 1970's. With the front tires set wide for rowcrop work, they were quick and agile pullers of knifing sleds, cultivators, and later, spray rigs. In their varied versions, they performed a multitude of tasks from plowing through planting and harvesting.

With the Popping Johnnies on the job, many was the time when the happy whistling of a farmer could be heard accompanying the rhythmic popping of the tractor.

In the fast-paced, computer-sophisticated world of modern farming, it is seldom that you will hear an operator whistling from the seat of their tractor. The dearth of popping tractors and whistling farmers are our loss.

For mainstay, start with an M—Farmall Model M. A lot of Plains cotton and grain country would never have become so productive without them.

M's purred like a contented cat while they disked and hoemed, shredded and planted, cultivated with puller and pusher tool bars in concert, stripped cotton, picked corn, pulled rowbinders.

What Plains farmer of any prolonged experience could forget the classic sounds of the bright orange Case wheatland tractors of years past?

Powerful engines hummed with authority, even picking up the cadence once the sun started down and the air cooled. They pulled sweep-and-drill rigs to get wheat into the ground during the fall, one-way plows and hoemes for summer tillage, they led breaking plows in round-and-round circuits either steered by hand, or following a furrow guide and "running wild," they rescued bogged combines and trucks during the wheat harvest.

There were many old tractors with their own classic sounds and personalities—features like screaming flywheels and hand clutch levers that invariably banged the operator in the kneecap, radiators that ran hot, butane fuel systems that sometimes froze up.

Some models had characteristic rattles, sometimes a piercing whine in third or fourth gear, or they might stutter a little as they poised for the jump to road gear speed. You want a sense of speed when roading a tractor? Just hop on a vintage M and ease back the throttle as it takes up the pace of fifth gear. Compared to today's tractors, you may not be moving all that fast, but it sure feels like it.

Not all that many years ago, one of the farmer's greatest tests of staying power was just getting one of these tractors started. Today, about the meanest test is paying for one.

Most of these jewels of a bygone era ran pretty well, once you got them started, but that was the catch. Plowboys grew blue and bug-eyed revolving the flywheel or spinning the crank handle to turn the motor over. A steady hiss emitted from the petcocks as compression built and blew away in fits of contrariness when the engine turned over but would not come to life.

Invariably, the hard-starters took the "studs" on a sweltering July afternoon when there were still 40 or 50 acres of maize to run the knifing sled or the cultivator through...There were frigid November, December and January mornings, too, when a man risked breaking off cold-stiffened fingers with the effort of rolling the thing over.

After a plowboy spun the flywheel or twisted on the tractor's starting crank for 30 minutes, amid fits of blind staggers, his tongue hanging out, it was as if the machine was taunting him when it kicked over once and quit.

Maybe that is why the forerunners of today's tractors sounded so sweet when they finally fired off, whether cranked with muscle power or electrical starting systems.

Coaxed to life, bygone tractors displayed personalities that will never be duplicated.

Hog Scaldin'

The hogs were committed, not just involved in these gatherings to work for a common purpose.

There was a time when the crops were in and a really brisk cold snap moved through causing neighbors to come together for "hog-scalding."

These were all-day gatherings at a central farm where there was water, a windmill tower to hang the hogs, and room to work.

The "host farmer" would dig a fire pit. The scalding vat was placed over it and filled with water. Old cedar posts fueled the water-heating fire that was lighted early on the appointed day.

Folks arrived in pickups dragging clattering stock trailers laden with huge hogs; red Durocs and orange and black-spotted crosses, white-footed Poland Chinas, dotted Spots, white-belted Hamps and black Berks with turned-up noses. These monstrous critters had attained size, over time, on a steady diet of ear corn and assorted cracked grains.

Wearing ear-flapped caps and bundled in coveralls and bulky sweaters layered over flannel shirts, early arrivers huddled around the fire. They waited for the steaming water in the vat to reach scalding temperature.

Men stood around, pocketknives in hand, spitting and chewing, shaving sticks, appreciating the fire's warmth. They listened to new stories, relived old ones, laughing loud and long and often.

These neighbors-in-waiting dressed their knives against oiled Arkansas stones, holding their knife blades at an angle and working them in a circular motion against the abrading stone to impart a keen edge to their working instruments.

Butcher knives would be constantly dressed during the course of this day.

Hogs were unloaded from the trailers into a lane of panels and herded into pens of wired-together wooden panels. Late arrivals were left in the trailers they had come in, where they rooted against the drums rolled into the trailers to crowd their passengers to the front end, against the chance of sudden weight shifts that could throw a vehicle out of control.

Some experienced soul would finally test the steaming water in the vat with a hand, inserting fingers, jerking back the appendage from the sudden heat and steam, and nodding that it was ready.

A couple of fellows would fetch .22 rifles, loading them with cartridges dug from shirt pockets. They would move deliberately to the edge of the pens, already selecting a hog even as they walked toward the panels. Squinting with concentration on the front sight stud at the end of the rifle barrel, they took careful aim for the flat area of the head between the ears. At the sharp crack of the rifles huge hogs toppled, stone-dead, felled instantly by brain shots.

Men rushed in to bleed the animals, grabbed the splayed legs of the felled hogs and made for the scalding vat.

The carcasses were eased into the hot water atop chains stretching across the vats. Men sawed the chains slowly back-and-forth, being careful not to let the carcasses slip off of the chains as they rolled the dead hogs in the steamy water. The rotating motion of the hog carcasses sloshed water over the rims of the vat and into the fire pit, to hiss against the glowing coals.

Scalded hogs were lifted out of the vat and set down by the teams of men working the suspending chains. Workers swarmed over the steaming carcasses. Fingers cupped around their tools, men went after the hair coat, scraping away the bristles. The hog carcasses were surprisingly white after the scraping was finished.

Singletrees from horse-drawn days were used in spreading the hind legs of the porkers and securing the hairless carcasses for hoisting on the windmill tower.

Once the work hit a rhythm, four or five hogs were hanging from the windmill at a time.

Skilled butchers gave their knives a quick dressing before opening the carcasses. Men with enamel pans and washtubs caught hearts and livers—fresh delicacies to grace supper tables.

Carcasses were cut into manageable portions, to be taken to a "salting shed" for further cutting.

Hog scalding continued through the morning. Flurries of activity were set in motion by the crack of rifles—like a starter's pistol triggering a race. It became sweaty work, despite the brisk temperature.

The dinner break was welcome when it came. Leaning against the walls of barns and outbuildings, the scalding crew made short work of what ladies had spent all morning and part of the previous night preparing.

Afternoon work shifted to the salting shed. Barrel and plank tables provided work space for those who generously rubbed sugar cure into cutup pork. Some workers cranked the handles of sausage grinders, mounding great batches of pork in huge tubs and working spices into the sausage by hand.

Some sausage was squeezed into casings, some left in tubs for attention at home.

The salting shed was crowded with neighbors working for a shared purpose. The sweet odor of sugar cure permeated your thoughts of those chops and hams and sausage and sides of bacon, all well-seasoned reward for the labors of growing animals at home and sharing the work of processing them.

The hog pens and trailers were at last, empty, the farm pickups cached with cargo of cured pork. The gathering broke up gradually, like it had come together.

Neighbors departed with jokes and smiles, handshakes all around, and a satisfied feeling of having worked together on a job important to all. Hog scalding was as much neighborly gathering as work session.

If you want to see a current-day example of the work or its trappings related to the old days of hog-killin,' you must visit the preparations for a grand event like the Umbarger sausage festival or the White Deer Polish sausage feed. Health regulations being what they are nowadays, folks who probably know way-better than the inspectors what is to be done at a hog-killin' aren't allowed to butcher their own livestock. That all has to be done by a licensed and inspected facility now—not that it makes the hogs any difference. They end up the same, regardless.

Before their big German sausage dinner at Umbarger, the good folks of St. Mary's still get down on their knees to mix their secret sausage recipe with hand and muscle motion, and to crank great trayfuls of sausage through the squeezers into casing. Elongated links of hand-cranked sausage then go to the church hall basement for slow cooking in roasters.

Sausage day at Saint Mary's is no gathering of neighbors around a friendly fire heating up a scalding vat on a cold morning. There is no scraping bristles, shoulder-to-shoulder, no hoisting hogs up on the windmill tower, no dressing pork with sugar cure. But here we still find a whole parish hall full of neighbors who continue to gather on a November day to prepare pork. The event is, in its way, a throwback, and a salute to the communal hog butcherings of another time. The cooperation and pursuit of common purpose are impressive to watch.

It is easy, now, to walk into a store, pick up a package of bacon or chops or ham and be on your way. No gathering corn from the fields, no forking feed over the fence to the hogs or lugging water to them in buckets for months on end.

Bringing home the bacon is a lot more convenient, and nobody much misses the hard work. There's not much feeling of neighborliness and accomplishment in picking up a package from the meat counter, though.

Livestock Teaches Life

Vital lessons of life—and its value—can be learned through working with livestock.

Our nation has struggled for some time now over the apparent desensitizing of children to death. The rash of shootings on school campuses has been particularly disturbing and perplexing.

Experts keep probing for causes of this malady, seeking ways to address it. Many are especially troubled over how kids can take a human life so easily.

I believe school kids all over this country—and we especially mean far-removed from-the-farm urban kids—could find vital lessons in life, responsibility, and respect by being involved in personally caring for livestock. This may sound like twisted thinking, but stay with me.

Kids of appropriate age learn a lot about the value of life and the realities of death when they are responsible for raising an animal eventually meant to serve as food.

We're not talking about pets. Nope, we're thinking more about a focus on the mostly unglamorous chores of having to feed and water, clean the pens, and tend to the health needs of livestock. These are chores to be performed morning and evening, every day, regardless of weather, daylight or dark. Getting these chores done whether-or-not it's a holiday or you feel like it, or despite the fact that you'd rather have your sister or your brother or your mother or your dad do it, because it's your responsibility. If you don't do it, critters are eventually going to wind up with four feet straight up in the air—not sunning their bellies—but because the poor beasts that depended on you croaked when you didn't handle your responsibilities.

We get sometimes-tough and very real life lessons having to nurse ailing critters through scours and chronic coughs and fevers and going off-feed, and facing the reality that sometimes, despite your best efforts to care for them, they die.

Livestock care reality is a lot different than the "virtual reality" of many video games. How real is this virtual reality when all sorts of shooting and stabbing, fisticuffs and blowing-up is portrayed by media as bloodletting without real pain, loss, or sorrow?

On the video game, television, or movie screen, violence seemingly happens in a vacuum.

Kids tending livestock realize a whole other reality.

When the animals these kids are responsible for die, they do not get back up again in a few minutes and appear in the next episode.

A lot of 4-H bucket calf project kids find out about being responsible for animals and death being a part of the equation at fairly tender ages. Seven-year-olds, and their older brothers and sisters can splash bucketfuls of love and affection on a bucket calf, right along with the milk formula they feed it via the nippled bucket, and the calves can still scour or have pneumonia, and, sometimes, die.

It's a hard lesson that children sometimes have to work through with the watchful help of their parents.

Work with livestock any length of time and some will become hopelessly ill. Fate may even decree, especially for lamb and hog keepers, that packs of marauding coyotes or dogs will attack your best-kept livestock and injure them terribly.

When you tend livestock daily you come to care about the animals. It is a bond hard to explain, but you understand, somehow, that sometimes the only right thing you can do by the animals when they are severely injured or deathly ill is to end their misery.

That is real, and it is hard. If you have to put down a pig or a lamb or a calf that you have wrapped a lot of your labor and caring into, you will struggle and agonize, and ultimately do it out of respect for the animal—but you will never do it lightly.

At young ages, a host of rural youngsters lucky enough to have already worked with livestock are keenly aware that you don't go around wreaking senseless violence on animals—or on people.

Somewhere in the process of caring for livestock you are also going to learn where food comes from—and it sure isn't the grocery store.

There is a far more real price of beef and pork and lamb, turkey, and chicken than the retail sticker on the neatly-arrayed packages in the frozen foods case.

Courage
and Sportsmanship

You can witness these fine traits many places in life—
including at the local livestock show.

From January through March in rural Texas the stock show season is underway. Youngsters and the young-at-heart who work with them harbor dreams of perfectly-fitted steers and lambs and hogs, and nabbing a top placing in the county show, or even the Holy Grail of the stock show circuit—a big win at the Houston Livestock Show and Rodeo.

Stock shows, properly handled and participated-in with the correct attitude, have long been a means of keeping the families interested in that sort of thing working together. As much work as is involved, you had best all pull together. This can teach young people responsibility, leadership, persistence, and yep, though not always acknowledged, courage and sportsmanship, just as in athletics.

The Hereford Livestock Show in my own community has offered many chapters in an ongoing saga of fine examples of some of these qualities displayed by the competitors, and sometimes, those working in the ring. The 2004 show was no exception.

There are differing opinions on the appropriateness of competitors aiding one another, or ring stewards lending assistance in the ring. I guess the competitive thing is at a much higher pitch in the major shows, but in my opinion, lending a helping hand is always appropriate.

Exhibitors and their animals can have bad days. Well-practiced kids can hit a tough spot. The best-prepared animal that has led or driven well in hours of practice may suddenly balk or blow up or run amok in the ring.

I don't know a lot about what criteria judges use to select showmanship winners, but I can remember a young man from years ago who would have gotten my vote.

He had been placed about midway down the class in the first sort-through by the judge. He was showing a lamb with short, curling horns, and was poised over the animal to set him up and provide the best presentation. Just as the boy reached down to position the animal's rear, the lamb jumped straight up and the critter's hard head sucker punched the youngster right under the chin, decking the kid like he had been hit by a linebacker.

The lamb hopped away and ran wild in the ring as the boy, obviously stunned and hurting, picked himself up off the floor of that grand palladium of community activities in a town named Hereford—the Bull Barn.

This youngster with tears in his eyes, a sore chin, and a headache, I'm sure, pulled himself together, moved quickly to trap the lamb in a corner of the show ring, and caught the ornery critter.

The boy quietly hustled the animal back into line and reset the lamb. The kid moved his head aside the second time the lamb tried the uppercut jump and resolutely set the lamb again.

Everybody in the barn could see that the youngster wasn't having what you would call a pleasant show experience, but he wasn't quitting. He kept right on showing, presenting his lamb the best way he knew how.

This kid was a definition of ram tough—to borrow a sales slogan from Dodge.

As I recall, this young man moved up a few places in the class. He certainly would have had my vote for showmanship.

During the 2004 Hereford show, the goat event offered examples of both courage and sportsmanship on the part of a couple of youngsters.

Almost-ten-year-old Marisa Bornemeier did really well in several classes. Getting several ribbons didn't come without some difficulty in the jumbo goat class, though.

Marisa was working with a jumbo goat that was probably twice her size and had an attitude.

As she brought the jumbo into the ring and was following the judge's directions to walk it around and line up along the north fence with the other contestants, the critter tried to take off. His abrupt shift and jump whirled Marisa off her feet and to the floor hard, but she held on.

She was hurt—probably had the breath knocked out of her—but no jumbo goat was going to make this girl cry. She gamely held on as the critter did its best to get her goat.

Ring sportsmanship suddenly changed everything.

Jordan Hicks, who had completed an outstanding senior season as a lineman for the Hereford Whitefaces the previous fall, threw a pretty effective block into the situation.

Holding his own goat with one hand, he reached out and nabbbed Marisa's goat by the halter with his other.

Muscling a little girl around was one thing for this jumbo goat, but there was no muscling Jordan. I could almost hear the burly football player whispering a warning to the goat to be still and play nice.

Once he snapped the goat back to attention and got it sort-of calmed down, Jordan called Marisa over, ever-so-softly said something to her, handed the critter back, and gently motioned Marisa to move her animal in line in front of him, where he could keep his eye on the miscreant goat.

I can't say that Marisa's goat was on its best behavior after that, but the good sportsmanship of a fellow competitor gave the girl the seconds she needed to collect herself, and she handled every trick the critter tried, even if she was gulping for air and shaking a little there for a minute.

Goat Showmanship results reflected courage and sportsmanship. Marisa was the junior Showmanship winner—and fittingly, I thought, Jordan Hicks won senior Showmanship.

Elephant Ears

This big-eared Poland China was a breath of fresh air at one wheeze-prone livestock show.

If your kid came sprinting up to you, wheezing, coughing, sneezing, and covered in talcum powder and oil, would you assume that they had been helping to change the baby?

Probably not, especially if this happened anytime from about January through March. The logical assumption would likely be that the kid was getting a critter fitted for the local livestock show.

For many years, stock shows bedded animals on wheat straw, and the use of such grooming accoutrements as coat dressing, shoe polish and talcum sprinkled liberally on the light-skinned porkers in the production was widespread.

I can't say that I regretted it when shows got away from wheat straw and began bedding animals either on wood shavings or sand. Initiation of the water-only rule for grooming with no coat dressing and especially no powder allowed, worked wonders to clear the air in the hog barn and in the show ring.

Many years have passed since I showed livestock. I still remember, and not fondly, how you pretty-much said good-bye to drawing another breath without wheezing for a couple of weeks once you walked into a stock show hog barn bedded with wheat straw.

Normally, you can't see the air you breathe—but we sure could see it in the hog barn, and it was no pretty spectacle, that choking cloud, hanging menacingly.

The chaff from the wheat straw spelled instantaneous lung lockdown. Once exhibitors started doping the Chesters, Yorks and crosses with talcum, the problem was more pronounced.

Even the thrill of making the sale didn't clear your lungs or your head, although if you did well enough in the sale, maybe your project would actually clear a few bucks that you could then spend on sinus and asthma medication.

A brief breath of fresh air in all of this came the season that I showed Elephant Ears, the Poland China with the enhanced audio receivers.

E.E. wasn't a bad pig, certainly not a great pig, just a big solid clunking hulk of ham and ears and personality that couldn't help the fact that a Hampshire had interloped somewhere in his supposedly Poland ancestry.

He had all of the markings of a Poland—except for those huge semi-upright ears—and those weren't his fault.

We got into the Poland class on the good graces of a sifting judge and then we never looked back.

I brushed him smooth with griddle brick, daubed the white shoe polish on the appropriate marking points on the legs and face, and left the dark areas slick and jet black with coat dressing. The old hog slicked-up right nice.

In the show ring he displayed his docile, amenable nature and worked those ears to maximum advantage. The girls pronounced him cute, some folks asked if he could fly, and ultimately, even the judge was impressed. On style and panache we managed to end up in the top end of our class—and in the sale. What more could any owner ask of his show pig.

Of course, the ugly word went around the ag shop the next week—something about there being a Hampshire in the hog shed, but mercifully, E.E. had his ears relaxed and didn't hear the pork roast...

He was over by the fence, being petted by the girls who still thought that he was cute.

I kept telling the girls that Elephant Ears was with me, but they were only interested in the hog.

What a ham.

Looky-Here

Some folks like to brag about their finds along the roadways and fields of life.

We probably ought not to call them junk collectors, to their faces at least, those folks who watch the ground around them and are forever picking up odds and ends in the fields and pastures and alongside the roadways. Whenever they find an item that in their estimation is of some worth, they exclaim, "Looky-here, what I found."

Amazing, the relics that a plow can turn up and these people can spot. Horseshoes, bits of harness, old plow bottoms, the fuel tank to an ancient white gas clothes iron, rowbinder sprockets, a piece of wagon wheel spoke.

Some people would just toss this stuff aside and go on, but the looky-heres just can't help picking it up. Not worth a whole lot, most of it, but good conversation pieces. If nothing else, looky-here folk get to ask unsuspecting bystanders if they know what this gadget or that is. They get to show off their unique brand of knowledge when nobody else has any earthly idea.

These "treasure hunters" may have the back of their pickup filled with their myriad finds...Pieces of chain, bolts and nuts, a perfectly good clevis. An assortment of wrenches that surfaced, rust-coated, from wherever it was that they went into hiding. Here's the handle to a hydraulic jack. Over there is the crank to an old tractor.

One fellow came up with almost a complete set of sockets, the ratchet, and the tool box to hold them, just because he was traveling the road at the right place and time. Cost him about two bucks for the one missing socket, and he had himself a full set of tools, just for keeping his eyes on the road.

A guy working for my uncle found a set of "spiders" from a rolling cultivator in the fencerow. Someone must have lost them while road-hopping a tractor and cultivator from one field to another.

Tooling along in the old pickup I came upon a rod and reel lying in the middle of the county road. Wasn't a soul in sight that it might belong to, or a vehicle to be seen that it might have fallen out of. I "adopted" it. Took some southern engineering to get the reel to work after it had bounced around on the roadway. The rod was okay and the price was right.

You'll sometimes see a single shoe lying in the road, but never a pair. Probably some looky-here type already picked up the other one.

I know of a guy who once stuffed an old coin purse that he was retiring full of paper and left it at a busy road intersection—a hoax on some looky-here that might happen by and get excited, thinking they had found a purse with a wad of cash in it.

Chisels, cultivator sweeps, hay rake parts, harrow spikes, great wads of wire and other jagged bits of metal sometimes protrude lethally from roadways where they were dragged to the surface by county maintainers blading the barditches alongside the road.

These wicked road hazards would gash the tires of unwary travelers but for the looky-here sorts. They stop, pick the offending item, throw it in the pickup bed and dust off their hands, figuring they will save some soul a disastrous blowout or rollover.

These good Samaritans of the roadway deserve to find a little worthwhile stuff awaiting rediscovery and recycling—like wrenches, chain, trailer pins, hoes, shovels, hubcaps, thermos jugs and five-dollar bills.

Funny how useful things are "lost" in the countryside. They leap away where you set up shop on the end of the field to effect repairs. This usually happens when you are up to your elbows in something that you can't turn loose.

Wrenches make the great leap from the toolbar of a plow, the cab of a tractor, the endgate of a pickup. They burrow into the soft earth, to hibernate until disturbed by plowing a few years hence. By then they are decked out in brown rust camouflage so only the looky-heres will find them.

I know a fellow who lost a pocketknife in a field, came along plowing that field the next year and found it. That is bucking the odds.

Rarely, the looky-here folks may be hoarding shards of primitive tools and utensils, flint arrow and lance points and scrapers, bits of mammoth jawbones, teeth and tusks, buffalo horn and skull fragments, spent casings from Spencer and Sharps rifles, uniform buttons, maybe even a rusted-out Colt's Army frame.

These are sometimes found by the most aware of this forever-searching lot, and the finders are duly proud of their treasures. Maybe unduly. We hear about their finds endlessly.

There is a time-honored response to looky-here artists if they brag excessively about what they have found.

Just say, "That looks exactly like one that I used to have."

The Great Spring Break Fishing Fiasco

Necktie parties were thrown for accused cattle rustlers based on less evidence than confronted five "fishing felons" on spring break.

Gloriously mellow spring days and incarceration in classrooms should not mingle. One beckons with warm sun and intoxicating moist freshness in the air, pledging between the blustering of March winds and fitful winding-down days of winter, new life and adventure outdoors. The other, in the confining halls of learning, demands attention to rote and writ, meter and matter. It compels notice of textbook and lecture, more than can sometimes be managed. Spring is not a spectator sport. Academia finally gives up and declares "spring break."

During high school days, our imaginations were fired by a succession of balmy days prior to spring break. To our sophomoric minds, mild weather meant that bass and catfish and crappie were surely on a feeding rampage somewhere. Our minds raced with the possibilities of dunking minnows, drowning worms and reeling in lunkers. The animated stories of one Ronnie Barham about a great fishing pond near Flomot, down in Motley County, fired us up. Ronnie had relatives there, knew most everybody and could get access to the pond. The "great spring break fishing expedition" was born.

Our "camper," was a set of cattle racks on the bed of a 1950 GMC pickup with canvas roll-down sides and top. A sheet of plywood suspended between lower bars of the cattle racks gave bunk space.

Five of us, Ronnie and Joe, Tony and Gary and me, lit out for the fabled Flomot fish tank, bent on hanging us a hawg. We camped beside the mesquite-surrounded pond that Ronnie guided us to.

We had decent luck the evening we arrived and catfish and frog legs sizzled in oil and cornmeal in a frying pan over a bed of mesquite coals. We went to sleep to fish tales, the rush of wind in the mesquite and the yodeling of coyotes over a rise.

Next day, having about worn ourselves out reeling in stunted panfish, we decided to run up to a little grocery near downtown Flomot.

We cast our fishing lines out, weighted the rods lest they be pulled in by some monster, gathered the camp loosely, and left the end gate to the cattle racks propped against a mesquite. No point in hauling it to town when we'd be right back.

Our lunch meat, candy bars and soda pop replenished, we returned a couple of hours later, expecting fish on our lines.—We caught way more than we figured on.

All of our lines had been reeled in. Standing amongst our possessions were two fellows wearing Stetsons and stern expressions. They were eyeing the cattle rack endgate.

Ronnie sidled over, asking/stating, isn't this old so-and-so's place, assuring them that he had permission to be here.

The strangers allowed that this had been so-and-so's place, right up until they bought it from him, months ago, but nobody had permission to be in here now.

In accusing phrases they told how a prize bull had disappeared only a couple of weeks ago. Tracks showed that the bull was loaded on a pickup, near this pond.

"You boys don't be in a hurry to leave. The sheriff will want to talk with you. We've already sent over to Matador for him," one of the cross-looking fellows said, helpful-like. The rifles in the rack in the back window of his pickup cab looked like cannons.

With sober stares, five spring break bass fishermen realized that they were busted. We were deep in the stuff of the meadow muffins littering the pasture about us.

We slumped on the pickup running board, awaiting our fate. Joe's wisecracks about how we would likely receive a free night's room and board at the "crossbar hotel," didn't help.

I watched the two Stetsoned strangers nervously. They didn't have a rope—at least weren't displaying it openly, but they sure were looking at a tall mesquite a lot. Tightness gripped my throat. Necktie parties had been thrown in "honor" of alleged rustlers on less circumstantial evidence than these guys had.

A car clattered down the pasture road, throwing up a plume of dust. It crept to a halt at the edge of the pond. A hefty fellow with a big badge on his shirt climbed out and looked straight at us. The dreaded, knotted-stomach moment had come. The high sheriff confronted the cutthroat crappie gang, cowering before the prospect of swift and terrible justice.

In panicked pondering of the finer points of the law, I fuzzily recalled my Dad telling me a few times that the lawman at Matador was once a neighbor, name of Spray, wasn't it?

"Are you Mr. Spray," I croaked weakly as the law approached.

He was, he said. Who was I, and what was I doing here? I told him my name and gushed our sad tale of lily-white innocence to his stone-faced, chin-rubbing listening. The high sheriff took it all in. I thought I saw a smirk.

"How the heck is your dad? I thought a lot of old Pete," the high sheriff remarked.

Our case recessed to the rear of the landowner's pickup. The law and the complainants kicked dirt, picked up bits of grass to chew, and deliberated at length. Their discussion was occasionally interrupted by choked-back laughter.

Solemnly, the jury came in at the front of the sheriff's car. We hard-bitten fish felons who had gone bad in the big pasture quaked in our boots before them, knowing that we could be headed to the big-house for our fishy dealings.

The law pronounced its verdict:

"I guess you boys just made an honest mistake, but you fellas can see how folks on this place would be a little touchy over an endgate in their pasture after somebody made off with their bull. You boys pick up and move on and there won't be any charges pressed."

We did, and they didn't.

Thus ended the great spring break fishing expedition. Our luck ran good. We caught a reprieve that was a keeper.

Like a Wave on a Slop Bucket

Waving is a friendly country tradition. Skip it, and you might be accused of high-hatting someone.

Waving, once a widespread rural custom, is still practiced some places, but this time-honored tradition seems to have faded.

Surprising, what some folks who do not comprehend the country tradition of a friendly greeting make of waving.

"Who was that you were waving at?" A city cousin or foreigner to the heartland poses the question while riding with you in the pickup. They notice that you have been waving at most every vehicle that passes.

"Gosh, I don't know. Somebody going down the road, I reckon."

"If you don't know them, why do you wave at them?" City-types demand a logical explanation to questions with the most obvious answers.

"No special reason. They just needed to be howdied."

A few inquisitors find this a satisfactory answer and leave well-enough alone. Others shake their heads, dismissing this waving stuff as another quaint habit of hayseeds.

Where the roads aren't heavily traveled, nor the population dense, farming neighbors wave at one another on the roads and at the field ends. It might be a while between seeing folks, so you howdy them. Not waving might be taken for high-hatting.

We farmed a place on the highway between Hart and Nazareth where traffic was steady. Turning the tractor or moving irrigation pipe and siphon tubes at the highway end of the field, we waved at passing motorists as we worked. Many passersby would turkey-neck, smile and wave back.

There are many styles of waving from behind the wheel along country roads. Animated, big-friendly, hand-waggling, grinning-from-ear-to-ear, stick-your-whole-arm-out-the-pickup-window waves come from many of the close neighbors as they motor past. These are "hundred-dollar waves."

Variations on one, two, and three-fingered waves are practiced. Some drivers lift the index finger of one or both hands above the steering wheel in a slight salute. Some lift the index and middle fingers. A few lift their hand slightly from the wheel and give a Boy Scout-style, three-fingered greeting. Occasionally you get a big flywheel back-and-forth motion of the hand, like the water cascading inside of a bucket when you use a circular sloshing motion to rinse it out. This is a greeting "as big as a wave on a slop bucket."

When I left the part of the country that I grew up in and moved to new territory, it was almost insulting to wave and be greeted with a questioning, stern stare. Apparently some people obviously lacking in country culture wonder what you want, or why you wave.

I have traveled all over the state reporting farm stories. Waving is done in some areas, not in others.

The harder that folks have to scrape to make a living from the soil, the more likely they are to give hundred-dollar waves.—Many even wave first.

With the exception of the home ground, I find that folks in the Rolling Plains, the Big Country and the Edwards Plateau are among the best at Texan roadway greeting.

The country of the big wavers usually harbors the friendliest, most down-to-earth people.

The friendly-waving folks seem to understand better than most that you may not be able to count on the weather, the crops, or the roadway, but you ought to be able to count on the friendliness of neighbors...Lifting a finger is the least we can do to show it.

As Silly As...

Many sayings are linked to animals, rural experiences, or practical measurements.

For decades I've heard my Dad refer to an essential farm fix-all—baling wire, as "Texas lacing leather." We certainly laced it around plenty of fence panels and items of farm equipment to effect a temporary or permanent fix.

One of my Dad's pet sayings through the years has been "as nervous as a pregnant mule in a pit silo."

We have to think this through, now. A mule might be a bit stirred-up over being stuck down there in a high-walled pit in the ground—one of those that ensilage is tightly packed into. Seeing as how the animal is a sterile hybrid, a mule would likely be understandably nervous over becoming pregnant. So, I guess this would be pretty darned nervous.

Here are a few more items we liken things to:

Happy as...a pig in the mud. This infers utter contentment.

Higher than...a cat's back. Usually spoken when referring to the outlandish retail price of something.

Colder than...a banker's heart. Trying to get financed will help you come to understand this kind of warmth.

Luckier than...a puppy dog with two tails. Puppies are always happy and tell you so with their tail wagging. This way, they can be twice as happy.

Prettier than...a speckled pup. Is there any critter cuter than a pup with speckles?

Rougher than...a cobb. This should be self-explanatory to anyone who grew up without indoor plumbing and a roll of Charmin.

Broader than...two axe handles. A unit of measurement to illustrate extreme width, as at a stock show, where a steer's rear end might be broader than two axe handles.

Hotter than...a two-dollar cookstove.

More brass than...a billygoat, as in, can you believe that woman? She's got more brass than a billygoat.

Slower than...molasses in January...or cold motor oil...or a seven-year itch.

    Tighter than...a wedge.
    As warm as...grandma's gravy.
    Colder than...a well digger's (insert choice of anatomy here.)
    As lively as...a filly on full oats.
    Lower than...a snake's belly in a wagon wheel rut.
    Madder than...a wet hen.
    As fine as...frog's hair.
    As sneaky as...an egg-suckin' dog...or a chicken-stealin' coyote.
    Crooked as...a dog's hind leg.
    As goofy as...a guinea.
    As messy as...a sow's nest.
    As hungry as...a she-wolf with seven pups.
    Maybe some of these sayings will have you grinning like...a jackass eating briers.

Home Remedies

A home-brewed "cure" can sometimes remedy an ailment—or scare it right out of you!

Rural communities are generally far from major hospitals. In the last few years, communication with central emergency receiving centers and helicopter ambulances have helped to put top-notch medical attention within easier reach.

Distance to medical facilities may be a daunting challenge today, but slow travel and limited technology made it a grave matter in times past.

Country folk have nearly always found themselves in a make-do environment. This has included medical care. Needs must sometimes be provided for using things readily at hand.

Practical ingredients for home medical care came from the garden and henhouse, the dry goods and hardware stores, pastures and river drainage breaks, and rarely, the drug store.

Foremost in rural medicine chests were coal oil, turpentine and kerosene—all purpose antiseptics and ointments used for cuts and abrasions. Youth with wounded extremities might be advised to dip them in coal oil. Amazingly, the damage often healed.

Kerosene was important in working stock. It kept surgical wounds clean, prevented swelling, sped healing and discouraged insects.

Epsom salts were, and remain, inexpensive relief for swelled, sore joints.

From the garden, garlic proved a natural antibiotic. Mustard, onion and garlic packs relieved congestion.

Onions and assorted hot peppers were thought to have powers over colds, sore throat, sinus and stomach maladies. Modern science has found that the capsaicin contained in jalapeno peppers is an effective treatment for arthritis, mouth sores, and may even prevent heart attacks.

Potato chunks drew out boils, as did a concoction of egg and salt, bound on with light fabric.

Common salt drew venom from mosquito bites and relieved sore throat or sore gums when dissolved in warm water and gargled.

Carbolic acid was used for toothache—possibly because it killed germs.

Certain concoctions may have scared illness from the patient/victim.

It is hard to contemplate a large spoonful of castor oil, cod liver oil, or elixirs of sulphur and molasses or cream of tartar as medicinal—except in helping one to decide they weren't sick!

Baking soda, that old reliable, extinguished heartburn, eased sunburn when added to bath water, and relieved the sting and itch of insect bites when made into a paste.

For sunburn, strong, dark tea was brewed, cooled and applied to ease the sting. This sounds harsh but it works—very painful sunburn can be relieved overnight by applying Mentholatum and sleeping on a wool army blanket.

The pantry yielded veterinary aid. Scouring bucket calves were treated by mixing flour in their milk formula. Chewing tobacco might be used to worm the family dog.

Indians reportedly brewed medicinal tea from smartweed. Stinging nettles were ground into viable treatment for allergies.

In a fascinating history of some of the first Spanish-speaking natives and settlers in New Mexico, Alfonso Griego, in his work, *Good Bye, My Land of Enchantment*, wrote of the many medicinal herbs and make-do practices used by these people.

Smallpox, measles and whooping cough were the most common diseases and residents dealt with the maladies through the help of medicinal plants and roots growing in the mountains and valleys.

Medicos (medics) *parteras* (midwives) and *curanderas* (healers) were all familiar with medicinal herbs thanks to the handing down of this knowledge from generation to generation. They gave away their medical services, never accepting a fee, but farmers and ranchers generally saw to it that they received a gift of livestock or food, or some favor.

Parteras brewed a special tea of *cilantro* (coriander) and *yerba buena* (mint plant) that they gave to newborn babies, a spoonful at a time, three times a day for their first three days of life. This prevented and treated colic.

Patients suffering from a cold might receive *remojos de pies*, a cold bath from the knees down. Care was taken that the patient not get chilled, and the patient was then sent to bed.

Sliced potatoes dipped in vinegar were placed on the forehead of a fever victim to help bring the fever down and relieve headaches. Cold and fever patients might also be given *atole*, a blue corn mush, to make them sweat out the cold, and to maintain their strength.

A *medico* might set a broken bone, then use a layer of *istiercol* (cow droppings) over the break and bandage it with muslin strips. Several layers of this treatment would serve as a lightweight cast that would allow the limb to be moved without dislocating the bone.

Summer months were a time to gather many medicinal herbs including *estafiate* (sage), *inmortal* (antelope horns), *garbonzo* (chickpea), and *cana agria*, a plant of the buckwheat family used for treating sore gums, pyorrhea, and as a gargle for sore throat, as well as a *curandera*-recommended agent to clean and tighten the teeth.

Tomatillo (bull nettles) was used to clabber fresh goat milk for the making of a fresh white cheese.

Amole roots and yucca roots made excellent shampoo and *contra yerba* (caltrop) was used to treat infections. *Ocha* roots were thought to be good for treating sores.

Pitch from a *pinon* tree, known as *trementina*, was used to make a fine *enserado*, or hand pomade, and fine leaves of spearmint herbs, the juice of *yerba del manzo*, a product of the "lizard's tail plant," and wax was concocted into a mixture excellent for treating chapped hands. *Trementina* was also used for removing boils or deep splinters from under the skin because of its drawing properties.

Honey and lemon juice have long been thought to relieve coughs.

Broth from boiling poultry and soup bones had mystic healing power over common colds, flu and body aches.

Peppermint relieved sore throat, sinus congestion and stomach maladies. Lemon drops soothed upset stomach. Vinegar might also help. Carbonated water and syrup used to formulate soft drinks settled the stomach.

A toddy of medicinal whiskey, hot water and sugar might be administered against severe cold or flu. Jack Roper, the paint horse man over Canyon-way, says he can attest to the viability of this "cure." He is a firm believer that an ounce—or is that two fingers—of prevention is worthwhile. He says he consumes the potion daily—as a preventive.

Isolated Plains residents short on cash and comforts had to do the best "doctoring" that they could with what they had.

Care lavished on a patient may have been as potent a healing force as the medicine. It gave comfort and reassurance to both patient and would-be healer.

Great healing power exists in what we might call "kindness of the kitchen." If there is, indeed, milk of human kindness, it is poured liberally from brimming pitchers in the kitchens where caring cooks practice the art of preparing recipes of benevolence. Cakes for celebration and recognition, cookies that say welcome and are a mainstay of church and school activities, soup for an ailing neighbor, a hot meal for a family with someone in the hospital, a casserole sent to feed body and soul in a time of grief. Thoughtfulness gets folded-in with the other ingredients as one of these dishes is prepared.

Doctors may not find the assertion clinically conclusive, but it is sometimes possible to cook up a cure for what ails us—or at least a kitchen concoction to heal the spirit when we are low. The magic recipe includes heaping measures of caring.

Windmill Adventures
Farm kids have always been ingenious at finding adventure and making their own fun.

Farm kids, through the generations, have been pretty ingenious at finding adventure and making their own fun—hazardous though it sometimes seems by today's standards. Most every farm kid has climbed on top of or jumped off something that was perilously high, or found all kinds of other adventures—driving red wagons down a ramp or jumping tricycles off the chicken house, riding the sucker-rod of the windmill, rodeoing on the backs of calves, sheep and pigs, roping shoates, crawling through culverts, climbing trees and outbuildings, swinging from everything imaginable.

Our neighbor, the late Roberta Artho, was the mother of ten children—six sons and four daughters. Imagine, if you will, how harried her days must have often been with that many hooligans running amok finding things to get into out in the farmyard.

Roberta had her child-raising trials, to be sure, but she also had eminently practical ways of dealing with "kid challenges."

During one of her hectic days, while bustling about the kitchen, Roberta suddenly noticed that two of her small sons, Duane and Harold, were unaccounted for.

She quickly searched the house. Coming up empty, she dashed outside. To her horror, she discovered that her AWOL youngsters had climbed the ladder on the windmill that supplied house water and were near the top of the tower.

Roberta was deathly afraid of heights. In her latter years she would not have even considered taking a ride with her son, Duane, in the enclosed, sure-footed safety of the bucket from which he works to repair power lines for Deaf Smith Electric Cooperative.

However, at this crisis moment in her life, motherly instinct trumped fear of heights when Roberta's wayward boys were atop the windmill tower. Since her husband, the late Elroy Artho, was out in the fields, she had to deal with this towering kid crisis herself.

I'm sure she swallowed hard, she may have even uttered a Hail Mary as she clambered up the rungs of the ladder, but she climbed that windmill tower, gathered one of the boys and escorted him down.

She made a second ascent, took another recalcitrant into custody and came down again.

Back on solid ground, Roberta admonished Duane and Harold to stay put and dashed off to one of the farmstead buildings.

She came back wielding a hacksaw.—I imagine that at this point things looked pretty rough for our boys, who had to be wondering if their Mama was really going to lay into them with a hacksaw!

The hacksaw was intended for the windmill ladder, however. She attacked the bottom rungs with a vengeance, quickly cutting temptation out of reach of at least the smaller offenders.

Duane assured me that while Roberta didn't use the hacksaw on them, the boys did have their—hearts—warmed over the tower climbing incident.

Elroy was puzzled when he went out to check the windmill that night and found the bottom rungs of the ladder missing. He offered little protest when Roberta explained why she was such a cutup.

The hacksaw didn't end all of the windmill adventures, however.

Elroy had brought home a small cargo parachute from his military service days during World War II. This device became the excuse for more high-rise adventure for the Artho farm youngsters.

Virtually all of the kids, at one time or another, tied the parachute to themselves and bailed off of the windmill tower. The windmill jumpers survived their skydiving adventures relatively unscathed, and they laugh about them now.—Apparently, parachute jumping from the windmill stretched Harold's body and made him taller than Elroy and Roberta's other children.

Elroy's parachute was a great play companion for the Artho kids. They used it to discover wind sailing, tying it to a wagon or a bicycle and opening it to a stiff breeze, to whiz down the county road.

Other adventures shared by Artho kids included leaping from the top of the angled barn roof into the haystack below.

With all of the aggravation the kids caused her with the thing, you would have thought that Roberta would have burned that parachute.

After her passing, when some of the kids were going through her things, they came across a package in a closet.

To their delight, they found that inside the package was their old friend, the parachute, carefully folded and stored.

Roberta just hadn't had it in her to throw it away.

Instant Replay

Two-a-days, and getting to play in a scrimmage, even for just a few downs, left their impressions.

The days of August and two-a-day workouts for aspiring football players usher in another school year. The spectacle and thrill of high school football stirs small-town Texas.

Football might be equated with religion in the farm and ranch country. The team is emblematic of community pride. Some sociologists liken football games to ancient fertility rites, the teams to the armies representing their communities.

Folks believe fervently in their Whitefaces, Longhorns, Bobcats, Swifts, Owls, Tigers, Lions, Bulldogs, Kangaroos, Eagles, Moguls, Matadors, Patriots, Chieftains, Steers, Mustangs, Jackrabbits, Antelopes.

You can tell a serious football town. The streets are lined with banners and flags in team colors on game day. It's standing-room-only in the stadium for home games. When the team travels to away-games virtually the whole town travels with them—the last one to leave can turn off the lights.

The true fans, who bleed in the school colors, pack in under the stadium lights of Friday night for raucous celebration of every big play, every score—whooping it up for the accomplishments of the best warriors of our village against the "lesser" warriors of other villages.

Farm town boys who have a hankering to do so get the opportunity to sacrifice their time and their bodies for a chance to be one of these community warriors, to test themselves, to be a part of a working-together whole—to don the instant buff-up of shoulder pads and helmet and be a football player.

I played at football only a little—just enough to get a taste of the pain and the pride, the intense emotions of fear and courage and the fellowship on the field and in the practices that comes with working with your teammates.

I can't eye a football workout today without it calling back sore muscles, "strawberried" knees, elbows and shoulders, assorted joint and extremity aches, pains and injuries, the ringing ears of a real blast of a tackle.

Just the talk of two-a-days can still make me feel the dread of searing heat, pervasive cotton-mouthed thirst and gut-wrenching wind sprints that were always reserved as the final torture capping every intensely physical workout.

What little football experience I had was not illustrious, but I can say I tasted of the game. Even for a cannon fodder squad member like me, the game had its moments.

I can't remember what community's team we were scrimmaging on a particular August day, except that our opponents had dark helmets. Our coach, the late Don Ewing, was a fair man who encouraged everybody. He gave us all at least a little playing time and that counts for an awful lot to a keen-on-proving-himself-and-belonging young man.

Coach Ewing sent all 100-plus pounds of me in as a defensive back on the left side of the field at some point in that scrimmage.

On the corner in front of me was Coach Ewing's nephew, Ronnie Barham, a neighbor who lived a couple miles down the road on the old Jim Brooks place. Ronnie and I had spent lots of time together hoeing weeds, changing water, hunting birds, fishing, throwing footballs. Ronnie was a junior like me, but he was a football "veteran," while this was my first experience. I was glad he was in there to help me.

The opponents broke their huddle, came to the line and Ronnie quickly turned and advised me to watch for a sweep coming our way. I don't know how he knew.

"You hit 'em high, I'll hit 'em low," Ronnie said, his wink reflecting amazing confidence. I nodded—like I knew what I was doing—put my mouthpiece in, and clamped down hard with my teeth, bracing for what was to come.

At the snap of the ball, the line exploded. I watched the opposing quarterback toss the ball to one of his backs, who sure enough, immediately looped behind his linemen, who were cutting ours down in a sweep escort.

The ball carrier made for the sidelines and turned upfield. Ronnie and I were suddenly on the "hot" corner.

Through the bird cage of my facemask, I could see Ronnie "breaking down" into his famous legs-cocked, arms-poised, tackle-ready position. If that ball carrier got past Ronnie, I was the last defender at the Alamo. I came up quickly—you've got to support your teammate.

I felt as if I was running toward the ball carrier in slow motion. At the bottom of the facemask-framed scene was the blur of Ronnie lunging at the halfback's legs. Higher in my field of view was the runner's purple-helmeted head, shoulder pad-armored body and arms cradled over the ball.

I closed the last few feet, my mind racing. *Don't duck your head. Look into the tackle.—Stop this guy for old Hart High.*

Honestly, I kept my eyes open right up to impact.

I crashed, shoulder, chest, and helmet, into the melee. Pads and helmets collided with a popping, thudding click.

We fell, tumbled, scooted, skidded endlessly.

An official's whistle sounded somewhere far away. We kept on sliding and sliding. I guess the sideline caught us and arrested the skid.

When I realized that we were finally motionless, I looked around to see if I really was still alive. There was Ronnie, a dopey grin all over his face, still firmly wrapped around the ball carrier's legs. *"Attaboy Jimbo, we got 'im,"* Ronnie bubbled.

I had somehow ended the ride perfectly astraddle the poor ball carrier's helmet, literally sitting on top of the guy's head!

The sideline was alive with teammates hollering shouts of encouragement and congratulations. They ran over, slapping Ronnie and me on the shoulder pads and helmets as they hoisted us out of this entanglement and shoved us out onto the field, encouraging us to get into another one.

Two plays later I could hear Coach Ewing hollering, but couldn't make out what he was trying to tell me. *Watch out for*...something.

The opponents had already snapped the ball when I realized that a towering receiver had split out wide and was running downfield, uncovered...on my side. The guy must have been seven feet tall.

I turned to go with Goliath. In my peripheral vision, I could see that the ball that was going to score a touchdown over my blown coverage was already in the air. I ran frantically, trying to close the gap, dreading the reprimand I was sure would come from the coaches when Goliath scored an easy touchdown.

That football must have been filled with helium. It floated forever. I got close to the receiver and frantically reached out a hand. Miraculously, my fingers shoved the bomb away. I didn't have a clue where the ball went. I was falling, and Goliath was still on his feet. Panicked, I wrapped-up Goliath's legs on the way down, just in case he had caught the ball. The pigskin fell harmlessly to the ground.

Ronnie hauled me to my feet and pounded on me. Teammates were all around, hollering and pounding. *Way to go! Way to go! Thought you were going to intercept it!*

That day, running all of those windsprints in the previous week's practices didn't bother me a bit.

A week later, in another scrimmage. I got sent in for a couple of plays. A running back broke up the middle, waded through our entire defensive line and linebacker corps, then cut toward my side. He had a leg-churning head of steam up.

I was the last man. I had a shot at him. *Don't duck your head. Look him in. Get this guy for old Hart High.*

I'll never forget that play—I missed the tackle.

The original version of this piece was awarded a first-place column-writing award from the National Newspaper Association.

Francie's Bread

Delivered in linen-wrapped loaves to family, friends, neighbors, clergy, medical and lawfolk, this was bread of goodwill.

It is fitting that we call sharing a meal "breaking bread." There is no more universal food. Whenever I think of bread, I have fond recollections of my late grandmother, Francis Davis Steiert, and her honest-to-goodness homemade bread.

I guess that Francie was famous throughout a goodly part of this end of the state for the melt-in-your-mouth loaves that she turned out of her oven. These were shared widely with people from all walks of life, ranging from Amarillo to Hereford to Plainview and points beyond.

I liked to walk into Francie's kitchen, and her pantry, too. They were all business, from the cavernous flour bin right down to the cabinets and crockery mixing bowls.

It took only one whiff of the air emanating from that warm kitchen to know that there was no place that you would rather be, nor anything that you would rather be doing than watching Francie make bread.

Even in her latter years, she would bake at least a couple of times a week. I've often wondered why she went to such trouble, but it probably wasn't trouble to her at all.

Maybe part of it was habit from feeding work crews that congregated on local farms to gather the bounty from the fields. Horsepower was literal in those days. Raw muscle was the means by which the work was accomplished. Whether the help was "neighbored" or hired, the noon meal was part of the compensation a laborer worthy of his hire received for the day's work. It was deemed a serious shortcoming to send working folks away from the noon break still hungry. The food might not be glamorous, but there would be plenty of it and it would fill a person up.

On the day that she designated for baking, it wasn't unusual for Francie to get up at 5 a.m. She would have several loaves rising in the pans even before young sleepyheads discovered that it was morning.

Usually I got to witness the second go-round. I would watch

spellbound as she tossed brownish whole wheat flour into her big mixing bowl and yeast that she had warmed in tepid tapwater.

I guess that it was her Irish that prompted Francie to keep a vegetable can filled with potato water for baking day. Many times I saw her pour this treasured water off of a batch of spuds she had boiled for dinner, remarking how she would make use of it later.

Omitting this Irish potion from her bread was sacrilege. Maybe that potato water was the magic ingredient that made her bread so good.

She would grasp the big mixing bowl under one arm, like a football or a watermelon, and work its contents with a huge wooden spoon. When the dough was getting about right she'd go over to one of the kitchen cabinets, produce a box of raisins and toss a couple handfuls into the mixture. Grandmas are big on raisins. A few more spins of the spoon and it was as mixed-up as it was going to get.

Later, bustling around the sink, she would take flour from a big can and toss a little on her bread board, then fling a batch of dough onto it. Her hands rolled and kneaded the dough until she was satisfied, then she shaped it into loaves and placed them in pans. These were put on top of the oven and covered with clean linen. The bread was allowed to rise before baking. Then, she would slip four or five loaves into the oven and magic would waft through the air.

Francie wasn't much on measuring spoons or cups. She went by "feel" and what "looked right," and it invariably was—the hallmark of an accomplished cook.

My Mom was much the same way about measuring for practical cooking, like making gravy. She knew how much flour to toss into the skillet to brown, then how much milk to pour directly into the pan, no measuring. When the spatula stirring was finished, the gravy turned out flawlessly.

Francie always scolded that it was bad for you to eat her bread while it was still warm, but it never killed me none. Anything that begged for a little butter and a hearty appetite like her bread did couldn't be too dangerous— even if it was still warm.

If it cooled off before you got to crunch a knife through the crust, the bread was super for soaking up gravy or spreading with preserves.

I came to understand why she baked often and in abundance. This was bread of peace and goodwill. She delivered it to many folks, often-times still warm and wrapped in linen, or in a rumpled-up brown grocery sack. This peace offering was shared with family, neighbors, priests and nuns, doctors and nurses, as a condolence offering in a time of grief, as a token of appreciation to deputy sheriffs, even as an incentive package to the wayward manager of "Monkey Wards" over in Plainview, when he had messed up an order and needed straightening out.

She kept several loaves wrapped in linen and stashed back in her pantry, so she could dole them out as "care packages" as she deemed necessary.

A big special house was required to harbor such a breadmaker. I guess that was part of the magic of staying with Francie. Her entire home thrived on the things that went on in her kitchen—baking bread, putting up preserves and peaches, tomatoes and hearty soup, making kraut.

At her passing, her open casket was placed for vigil in the big east bedroom of her house—just down the hall from the pantry where the bread boxes were on the top shelf and linen that had held her bread offerings was folded away neatly in drawers.

Folks who had shared her life and her bread of peace came to pay respects. There were farm folk and store clerks and nurses, and a whole car full of nuns, looking like some great flowing black-and-white wave washing over the place. Seems so fitting that many lingered to visit over coffee and cakes and bread in her kitchen.—She'd have liked that.

Her house was quiet and empty for many years, save a few times when visiting family members might sleep there for a few nights.

The time came when, in an estate settlement, the house was sold. All of the bricks were removed from the exterior, the structure jacked up off of the great concrete porches and the sprawling basement that was dug with mule power and the onetime landmark hauled away on the beams of a moving truck. The house of great stature surely shrank

To this day, I can drive past the place where her house stood and it is not at all hard to close my eyes and see Francie bustling around the kitchen, up and down the stairs to the basement, wringing her hands, turning loaves from the pans to cool so they could be wrapped in linen, slipping a bowl of milk out the screen to a plump yellow or gray-and-white cat sitting on the window ledge.

In this day of synthetic everything, when there's only a few cents worth of wheat flour in a loaf of bread—that doesn't have any character—it's good to recall the magic of Francie's kitchen and the love that flavored her bread.

In our own kitchen, we see a wee bit o' the Irish blooming. Forgive me if I get a lump in my throat as I watch our daughter, Jaime, stirring raisins into the dough of her whole wheat rolls with a big wooden spoon—I think I saw her pour spud water in there.

Pie Power

Good pie is a square deal in the round.

Pie is enumerated among the great culinary delights. A whiff of pie warm from the oven rivets the attention of young boys and old men. It can antagonize pilferage when left unattended on kitchen counters with no one to answer the important question— is this just a pretty for us to look at before it goes elsewhere, or is it to eat?

Golden crusted, filled with temptation, pie has an awesome power to please. A hefty wedge can draw farmers and truckers and cowboys, phone repairmen, even bankers, to the local greasy spoon from distant fields, highways, pastures, job sites and ponderings of compound interest.

They'll make a pretense over chicken fried steak first, but it is the pie that they have been tasting in their minds and have their mouths all set for.

Because its making requires much effort on the part of the cook, good pie carries a subliminal message with every bite: "You are mighty lucky that somebody has gone to all of the trouble to make this."

Pie-from-scratch evolves from intense and caring hand labor that fashions fine crusts from shortening and flour and water in a flour-dusted workspace.

Into delicately sculpted crusts go honest ingredients: Butter, sugar, milk, eggs and cinnamon, apples, pineapples, blueberries, peaches, coconut, cherries, lemons, pecans, pumpkin, rhubarb, chocolate, bananas, cream, even unlikely things like buttermilk, cottage cheese and vinegar.

Some ingredients are topped with meringue to add a finishing touch to the pie. Others mate well with ice cream, whipped cream, cheese, when the golden wedges are cut from the round pan.

Light, flaky pie crusts that melt in your mouth are great art in their own right.

In a pinch, there is nothing wrong with pie that gets prepared in a ready-made crust from the freezer section, or from dough sticks. If that is what it takes to get pie on the platter, so be it. Pie in most any form beats no pie at all.

Suzanne Stevens once gifted us with a buttermilk pie. Seemed a strange thing to make a pie from, but then, I have heard about cooks on cattle drives making vinegar pie and some folks used to eat cottage cheese pie. The aroma of Suzanne's still-warm buttermilk concoction was overwhelmingly tempting. Feeling as we do about pie, we gamely tried it and awakened to a whole new appreciation for culinary possibilities for buttermilk—besides sipping and as an ingredient in biscuits and pancakes.

Suzanne's pie was the fruit of a recipe that came out of the Muenster country where she grew up. The native daughters of Muenster know a thing or two about turning out great pastry. Suzanne did her heritage proud.

Thanks to Suzanne sharing her recipe, buttermilk pie gets made now at our house. It has become a tradition right along with pumpkin pie every Thanksgiving. Dad and daughter and Granddad jockey for the choice pieces.

For my money, it is pretty hard to beat all-American apple pie for enjoyability. It goes well hot or cold, with ice cream or without, and the right kind of cheese alongside really brings out the flavor. It is eminently consumable.

Though it comes from the oven in the round, pie is a heckuva square deal.

Country Cafes

You can get a good chicken-fried steak and the local scoop.

Those who have misspent their lives in the big city have missed out on a colorful side of Americana if they have never slid into a split vinyl booth or a wooden bench for dinner in a country cafe.

They are the poorer for not having experienced places like the Green Frog or the Tip Top in greater metropolitan Hart, Ann's Steak House, just across from the courthouse square in Dimmitt, or Irma's on the corner of the gin yard at Lazbuddie.

All of those establishments are gone now. They were places where the waitress called you "hon," your coffee cup or tea glass was never empty and good customers could run a tab.

We can still enjoy classics such as Wanda's Dawn Cafe, right off Highway 60 in the big city it's named for. For many years in the small farm country there were Dairy Queens that were local institutions and made this honor roll, like the one that came to suburban Lorenzo through the sheer letter writing insistence of locals who wanted an eatery in their town.

There was a down-to-earth model in neighboring Crosbyton, too. The Dairy Queen at Olton and in dozens of other rural communities proved not only a choice spot at noon, but doubled as an unofficial senior citizens center.

In Matador, you angle parked your pickup in the middle of the street about a block from the Motley County courthouse and strolled into The Pizza Box, where you walked up to the counter, placed your order and fetched your own drink and silverware.—You could get all sorts of food, not just pizza, brought out to you when it was ready.

Down the road and across the Pease River at Roaring Springs, the Cafe R.S. served up a fish fry that drew them from miles around on Friday nights. At Chillicothe, a rambunctious Lions Club took over the local beanery one day a week at noon. Similar activities happen with various civic clubs and eateries in rural communities across the state.

Over at the Tulia Livestock Auction, there was a cafe adjacent to the sale barn. The coffee and burgers were hot, the conversation lively and on sale day, you could hardly stir the patrons with a stick.

From the tip of the Panhandle through the Rolling Plains, out west to the sprawling Trans-Pecos and on into the rolling Hill Country, there are untold numbers of "Cattleman's Cafes." They bespeak their clientele and mostly offer good food.

The so-called "greasy spoon" diners that dot hundreds of tiny rural communities have long done their part to keep the threads of the nation's heartland interwoven. They generate a unique sense of identity in the little towns and the surrounding countryside.

Country cafes are the natural gathering points for morning coffee and conversation. Diagrams of inventions, off-the-cuff accounting, quaint road maps and farm layouts are scrawled on napkins. Such figuring can only be done atop tables given texture by grains of salt and sugar spilled by the patrons.

Inspiration so great that it must be etched on napkins probably would never come if not for the atmosphere lent by the consumption of great quantities of steaming coffee from brown mugs with protruding spoons. Healthy skepticism spoken openly by throngs of onlookers and abundant horse laughs accompany the drawing and doodling.

Country cafes do the nation a great service. Within their confines, days of work get lined out—sometimes. Sitting around one excessively could get an individual labeled a "windshield farmer." Sins of crooked politicians (and coffee shop patrons know that all politicians are crooked) are enumerated and punishment befitting the crimes is wished for. The nation's economic woes are cussed, discussed and common-sense resolutions proposed.—If only the policy makers would listen.

The home team and the Cowboys are steered toward winning seasons, bugs and weeds are vanquished, calves and crops, children and grandchildren are spoken of long and often, and the fine arts of humor, embellished storytelling and country philosophy are much-practiced.

A placard declaring the establishment's support for the home team is taped to the cash register. Plaques on the walls declare that noon Lions, Rotarians or Kiwanians meet hereabouts on Mondays, Tuesdays or Wednesdays. Sometimes a clock with several revolving boxes around it is hung behind the short order counter. The spinning boxes advertise the local dirt contractor, Ace's handy dandy realty and the Johnny Pop implement dealership.

You can tell it's a real country cafe when the regulars walk in. They wave to the cook, maybe even poking their head through the kitchen door to holler "howdy" as they step around the counter to pour their own coffee or tea.

Regulars settle with easy familiarity, knowing most everybody in the place and greeting them all, then giving a thorough once-over and a nod to those that they don't. They will talk to you, even if they don't know you, if you speak "country friendly."

Country cafes are unofficial news bureaus. You can get an update on how much rain fell last night, the status of the cotton stand, how many steers got loaded on a semi—even how much Henry's new grandchild weighed, just by listening.

The regulars often sit at a common table. This table must be sturdy enough to hold up scores of elbows, the intricate diagrams of the napkin scrawlers and all of the bull that morning and afternoon coffee drinkers and the noon dinner rush can lay on. Regulars pay out one another's coffee.

Country cafes serve real food. It is honest grub—the kind that sticks to your ribs, puts heart back into you on the tough days and keeps working folks going. They have lunch specials. Chicken-fried steak smothered with gravy is mandatory. There may be other options like barbecued tips, fried chicken, meat loaf or liver and onions. On the side will be mashed potatoes, corn, pinto beans, cornbread or biscuits, and cobbler, a square of cake, or pudding for dessert.

Country cafe hamburgers are the two-fisted kind that come in a basket along with crispy brown french fries piled in deep layers. None of the stale heat lamp-warmed stuff of the fast food joints here. You can hear your order cooking on the grill. Nobody is going to go away from one of these places hungry. If they do, it is their own fault.

Come coffee time and at dinner, you will see lots of farm pickups and trucks bunched around. Footwear propped beneath the tables is mostly cowboy boots and brogans, although ersatz tennis shoes have come into the picture.

Farmers and cowboys, trainmen, utility linemen, oil jobbers, truck drivers, parts men, the local filling station operators—all know a good deal. The dinner special at a country cafe is still one of them. It is to their credit that country cafes draw working class.

You might see muddy irrigation boots piled at the door of a farm country cafe, to avoid tracking in mud. Such considerate action and steady patronage win their owners their favorite homemade pies on a regular basis.

When the rain or the snow falls and the patrons file through the doorway with a smile or a worried look on their faces, you'll find the linoleum mud-tracked. The customers try to scrape off the worst of the mud before stepping inside, but it still walks in. Country cafe proprietors understand. They sweep and mop and go on, figuring that the dirt will be good for their flowerbed.

Over at the Dawn Cafe, you might luck out and catch Wanda on a day when she's baking. She might bring you a whopping piece of cake, still warm from the oven, or a piece of pie, just as you are polishing off one of her Wandaburgers.

During December, Wanda comes by your table offering peanut brittle from a tin, even if you only bought a hamburger. She makes it in big batches just for the holiday customers, because they are special and she likes them to know it.

Sometimes she gets in an out-of-towner spouting blue language inappropriate for her establishment, or worse yet, bad-mouthing her Dallas Cowboys. She informs such offenders that "we don't talk that way about the Cowboys around here."

I saw her quiet down a fellow maligning the silver-and-blue with just those words one day. He hushed like a schoolboy who had been whacked with a ruler.

When he finished his cheeseburger, Wanda gave him some peanut brittle.

He left a tip.

Batchin' Hotcakes

Stir up a batch of this fend-for-yourself batter and you'd soon have hot blankets ready-to-go.

Friday nights and sometimes, in cold weather, we would have "bachelor hotcakes." These were a standard supper menu item when the ladies were gone and the fellows had to turn out something for table fare.

Dad, an expert in bachelor cooking, had a from-scratch recipe in his head that I finally wrote down:

HOTCAKES

In a large pot with a long handle, combine:

* One-and-a-half sifters of white flour, figuring a sifter at about two cups.
* A good handful of cornmeal, preferably white, if a grit-like consistency is desired.
* Half a cup of sugar
* One teaspoon of salt
* One tablespoon of baking powder

Stir all of these dry ingredients together thoroughly. Add enough milk to bring the batter to the desired consistency.

At this point, add:

* Two tablespoons of melted grease (an unpretentious bachelor-cooking term, because any cook measuring by ham-fisted handfuls should not use sissy terms like polyunsaturated cooking oil.)
* Two eggs well-beaten—or skip the grease and use more eggs.
* One teaspoon of vanilla
* Three drops of maple extract flavoring

Mix the batter well until it is a consistency that allows it to be poured or ladled into pans.

This makes enough batter to feed your people and anybody else who might show up, with a good chance of batter being left over for the next day.

Bachelor hotcakes are cooked in a pair of greased skillets, preferably well-seasoned with prior cooking experience, and placed on butane-fueled burners set at medium heat. Burning a few cakes may be required to learn correct cooking times.

Using one of the smallish ladles like you might put on the kitchen table, ladle hotcake batter into center of skillets, pouring one to three ladlefuls, depending on size of ladle and whether silver-dollar, medium or kitchen plate-sized hotcakes are desired. Batter should flow from the ladle and hiss like lava when it hits the skillet. Fizzles should appear around the edges of the cakes as they begin to form-up with the heat.

(HELPFUL HINT: Cooking of hotcakes is most successfully performed by leaning against the cabinet at the kitchen sink, in close proximity to the stove. Hold the spatula in the right or left hand, according to preference, with the thumb of the other hand hooked in the hip pocket, and one leg cocked slightly across the other.)

When the surface of the cakes is covered with air bubbles, slip the spatula gently under them and flip the cakes over, one frying pan at a time. As timing improves with experience, cakes will be a nice golden-brown on the cooked side as they are turned.

If you are an adventurous cook, and cakes are sufficiently done, you may pick up the skillet by the handle, using a hot pad, and attempt to flip cakes without using a spatula.

(A POINT OF ETIQUETTE: It is advisable not to serve hotcakes that flip onto the kitchen floor to company, unless the floor has been swept or mopped within the last week and the company being served is family or close neighbors. However, it is perfectly permissible for the cook to retrieve any misflipped hotcake from the kitchen floor for his own consumption, or to toss to the pot-licker dog in the back yard. Should the latter be done, it should be at the cook's and dog's mutual discretion. Any dog given hotcakes should make a game attempt to consume them, so as to avoid inferring to the flipper that a self-respecting dog would not eat his cooking.)

Once hotcakes have been successfully turned with the spatula, or flipped, allow an appropriate amount of cooking time, remove from pans, stack on plates and serve immediately, hollering, " I've got a couple of blankets ready to go!"

Move quickly to keep skillets greased and re-battered before they get too hot. A certain amount of smoke in the air, less-than-elegant dining, and some dirty dishes stacked in the kitchen sink are appropriate to the bachelor kitchen motif.

(ANOTHER HELPFUL COOKING HINT: Variations of the standard bachelor hotcake formula are possible. Add leftover red beans to batter immediately after it is poured into skillet to yield hotcakes with cowboy strawberries. For corn hotcakes, add leftover kernel corn. For cakes with cackleberries, fry up desired number of eggs in one of the skillets after a good stack of hotcakes have been prepared.)

Batchin' hotcakes are satisfying, quite filling and can be fun.

They can be lifesaving food. I remember a blizzard on the Friday before Palm Sunday, years ago, when a cowman who was hauling a trailer full of calves got "whited-out" by the howling weather as he was passing our farmhouse. He made it to our door.

He was warmed and reinvigorated with a stack of batchin' hotcakes and hot coffee and waited out the wind at our kitchen table until it declined enough that he could see to drive again.

He survived the potluck fare of our shifting for ourselves.

Ears of Summer

One of the finer celebrations of sure-enough, school's-out-forever summertime is a roasting ear slathered in butter.

Several years back, one of the local farmers explained to me, only half jokingly, that the trick to growing good corn in this country is to put a catfish at the head of every row. Not for supplying fertilizer Pilgrim-style, but as a nonelectronic moisture sensor to indicate when it is time to irrigate.

He said that if you run water down the furrows often enough to keep the catfish alive through the heat of the summer, you probably have watered your corn sufficiently to make a pretty decent crop.

I am not sure what it was supposed to have meant years ago when my Dad was irrigating grain sorghum with water from a lake and the furrows were literally swimming with waterdogs and umpteen thousands of little catfish sucked up by the lake pump. Some of the catfish fry managed to travel a full circuit from the lake through the flow pipe, into the ditch and down the hillside sorghum patch, then back into the lake again with the spill-off water. I don't recall if we harvested a binbuster grain yield, but certainly we had plenty of little moisture sensors wiggling down the furrows. I guess we were doing okay, had we been watering corn.

Among the finer assurances and celebrations of sure-enough, school's-out-forever summertime are roasting ears that come off in the days of the season in its stride.

The first sweet corn is gathered while still in the tender "nubbin" stage, collected in armfuls by irrigation-booted farmers who hustle the ears to the house just long enough ahead of noon to make it to the dinner table.

Youngsters around the place are enlisted to help with shucking and silking the sweet corn. This job is usually performed in the friendly shade cast by some handy tree around the homestead. The trimmings are piled in a box, wheelbarrow, or red wagon and a pan or pot procured from the house to put the corn in.

This is happy work. Kids generally consider field-fresh corn on the cob quite a treat. Shucking a few roasting ears is not unlike unwrapping birthday or Christmas gifts. Roasting ear shucking styles vary widely. Some peel away the shuck a layer at a time, prolonging the suspense of the ritual, while others go at the job much like peeling a banana, ripping off shuck, silk and all in narrow strips.

Each ear holds adventurous possibility. There is always a chance that young hands may peel back layers of leafiness to disclose the presence of squiggly earworms. These are to be shrieked over and their "grossness" remarked upon while unwrapping the prize.

Some older member of the crew wields a knife to whack off the silk and stalk ends of the ears, and to perform the milky surgery required to carve away the wormy spots. The knife person will have milk from the ears spattered all over their face.

Silks are an object lesson in persistence. They obstinately cling to the ears, defying the efforts of fingers to remove them. Silking the first roasting ears of the season is an impatient undertaking, a hit-or-miss proposition. The idea here is to pluck away the thickest of the corn's "hair coat" and get on to shucking another ear, hopeful that some inspector in the house won't nitpick over what's been missed.

A quick wash job at the kitchen sink disposes of more of the silk and the roasting ears go into pans of boiling water. This should not be a prolonged dunking. Don't want more than a mild scald or the kernels will be tough. The roasting ears are done just as soon as you can poke a kernel with a fork and it doesn't squirt.

Steaming ears are brought to the table, doused in butter and sprinkled lightly with salt.

Consuming this delicacy from the cob is an honored ritual. Unfortunately, it is necessary to cut the kernels away from the cob for snaggle-toothed six and seven year-olds, since they have no front teeth to get at them. The corn tastes as good, but is not nearly as much fun to eat when divested of the cob.

Roasting ears are the golden sweet, butter-dripping good stuff of summer, tasting of sunshine and freedom.

Eat heartily of the sweetness of this corn while it is fresh. Alas, the days of summer are numbered. School bells will ring again. Slathering up another roasting ear with butter should help to keep school days at bay a little longer.

Scent-Sations

Olfactory recognition can bring back things otherwise unremembered.

They come to us in a sudden rush, delightful old friends that had gone too long un-recalled. Olfactory joggings of our memory are vague, evasive, yet thoroughly familiar challenges to our recollection.

Our nose recognizes distinct aromas that made their impressions upon us in times past and the memories come flooding back.

Picking up hardware items in a huge building supply store, a forklift backs down a wide aisle, its reverse-gear alarm beeping. The forklift zooms past, hoisting a stack of boxes to an upper shelf. As it passes we get a whiff of something we know that we ought to recognize but cannot place. This lack of recognition bugs us so much that we stop in our tracks.

The forklift passes again. We see the small cylindrical fuel tank on the back of the contraption and that odor is there again. Recognition is sudden, distinct, relieving. The unmistakable scent trail of burned butane fuel exhaust from the forklift calls back the days when every tractor on the place ran on butane. We are in the tractor seat on sweltering summer or cold winter days when the heat from the engine was thrown back over you, pushed by the whirling radiator fan.

Driving with the windows down and passing a roaring well motor, there is no mistaking the hot exhaust-and-oil odor of summer irrigation season. Back come summer days of irrigating corn and sorghum, carrying armloads of muddy irrigation tubes, shoveling rows, setting ditch stops. The scent of moist soil and new canvas is married to the ditch stops.

The earthy smell of the summer's first run of potatoes, fresh-washed and put up in burlap sacks brings back vivid pictures of the old Hill packing shed next to the railroad tracks near the Farmer's Grain Company in Hart, when the spuds were loaded onto refrigerated boxcars.

Kerosene's odor reminds of its many familiar uses at the farm. It is a staple fuel for emergency light, even in an age of electrification. Many times, if not for kerosene lamps, the family would have been in darkness when electric power from the rural cooperative over at Tulia was interrupted in summer or winter weather. Clear-globed lamps wafting the essence of the amber fluid and wick-within-their-base provided defense against the dark.

The same lamps gave light in the cellar for work, storm shelter and warmth to stave off freezing of the canned goods stored down there.

Cottonseed cake's sweet-scented appeal reminds of feed rooms and barn alleyways and carefully-stacked 100-pound burlap bags of the squarish cubes in old boxcars that served as storehouses. Burlap bags of cow cake afforded seats in the back end of the elevator feed store while men shot the bull. More than a few times I wondered if those cubes really tasted like cake to the cows and if something that smelled that decent might be good for people to eat. Smelling cow cake calls back driving the pickup in "granny gear" with the hand throttle set on slow creep while Dad dumped cubes on the ground, or Granddad's old fishing bus, replete with stove and small kitchen table, where he mixed cake cubes and unknown ingredients into a lethal-looking concoction that he cooked on the little butane stove in a red-and-white pan he'd swiped from grandma's kitchen. He called the cottonseed cake-based formula "crab-bite." It was potent dough bait for catfish and carp that he angled after at Buffalo Lake.

The pungency of burning cedar brings back a hundred campfires fueled by old fenceposts—branding fires on rangeland, cooking fires on sandy stretches near the water crossings within Palo Duro Canyon or along Buffalo Lake's shore, where kids cooked wieners and marshmallows skewered on coat-hanger wire over glowing coals.

The acrid essence of gun oil and spent .22 casings reminds of the excitement when Dad let me shoot my own new rifle at a big red coffee can for the first time...Cottontail rabbits were "big game." Favorite colors became the green-and-red of a box of Remington or the yellow-and-red of a box of Winchester long rifle cartridges. Dad bought me a whole carton of Winchesters at Lon Brockman's seed store to feed the well-oiled single-shot rifle. The wisp of powder smoke that curled from the spent cartridge when I jacked the bolt open made an indelible olfactory imprint.

I can smell hot coolant and immediately go back to a sweltering June afternoon of rotary-hoeing maize with a Massey Ferguson 65 that was heating-up, halfway through the field. Coolant swelled and ran out around a radiator hose fitting. Dropping a gear kept the engine RPM up and made the fan spin faster to cool the Massey down.

A little washing gas sloshed on pants or shirt reminds me of a late uncle who always smelled of this bi-product of tinkering with and tuning tractors and irrigation engines.

Faint mothball scent brings back the porch and pantry that opened into Grandmother's basement and kitchen doors.

Just-cut forage conjures up rowbinders and bundles of redtop cane on flatbed trailers, or standing in shocks in the field.

Opening a carton of buttermilk, the first whiff is a throwback to turning the handle on a churn and drinking from a jar a rich potion dotted with butter flakes.

Breezes freshen and fade, bearing bouquets of memory. And so it goes. The nose knows.

Comfort Food

While it may not suit nutritionists or diet police, this fare is real, and sustains and uplifts through difficult times.

The family had spent most of the morning and afternoon dealing with endless details—papers and arrangements and decisions, getting the casket piece squeezed into the back of the car and 40 miles down the road in time for the arrival of the hearse bringing Mom home to the Holy Family Church for the vigil service to be held that evening.

In the interval between the four o'clock homecoming and the 7 p.m. vigil, we found a brief window of time to scatter to the family farm.—Home—to regroup and prepare. We did so, tired and famished.

Neighbors who hadn't caught us there had just walked right in the front door of the folks' house, leaving gifts. Life remains civilized enough that folks still do things that way out in the rural heartland.

Scattered through the living room and den were numerous flower arrangements. On the brass table just steps from the front door was an aluminum foil-covered pie pan. I picked it up. It was still warm from the oven, its contents perfuming the air with the odor of apples and cinnamon. There was no card to let us know who had left this gift. I guess its preparer knew we would figure out that the pie was a token of sympathy and condolence.

Sprawled across the top of the stove and the kitchen counters were pans of enchiladas, chicken casseroles, sliced ham, barbecued chicken, brisket, assorted loaves of bread, most with notes or some remembrance attached. Here before us was a spread of "comfort food" to sustain and uplift. Folks had been bringing it by in flurries for the better part of two days. They cared. They cooked.

Nutritionists and diet police cringe every time they hear the term "comfort food," getting all worked up at the idea of starches and sugars and calories.

Yet, in a time of trial and grief, you want some starch, you want to taste the real and right and familiar flavors of life, you need the energy locked within food made by caring hands to help you stand up to it all. It's remarkable how many folks still understand and remember this country tradition.

The whole of our family fell upon the offerings of consolation on that evening, drawing will and strength from noodles and chunks of chicken, spicy bits of beef and cheese rolled and baked in tortillas, the toasty, soul-warming tanginess of apple filling tucked into a flaky crust.

We shared, we appreciated and we were renewed.

After the funeral services the next afternoon, we and a company of friends and neighbors retired to the Senior Citizens Center within walking distance of the little community church. There in the kitchen were the ladies of the Holy Family Church's funeral dinner committee, headed up by Patti Hochstein Kern, one of the neighbors I wrote about when she played high school basketball. Patti and the ladies of the committee all had families and lives and things they needed to do, but that didn't stop them from taking the time to make sure that hot comfort food was waiting for us again—roast beef and mashed potatoes and gravy and green beans cooked slow with real bacon, homemade bread and rolls and cheesecake and blueberry crisp, and even a cobbler made with real rhubarb.

Kitty Crider, in an excellent piece in the Austin American-Statesman that I saved from years back, says funeral food is important for the messages that it conveys. It speaks on behalf of its preparers, letting the recipients know that its giver feels their grief and shares loss and a moment with the family. While the food preparer may be worried about having the right words to say, their food speaks volumes, expressing a sense of commitment, a message of compassion through toil.

You never appreciate neighbors so much as when you need them. Their message of condolence is never so well expressed as in the comfort food—the bread of compassion—that they share.

Small Town

It's okay to be "small town." No need to apologize.

Some people and places stuck on themselves label the rural heartland "small town."

That was once an utterance of uppity contempt. In these times it may be not so much an insult as an expression of envy.

It's okay to be small town. Don't even think about apologizing for it.

I don't know that we have to make amends for being from a place where you can walk into the post office and fellows still hold the doors open for the ladies, or help when somebody's carrying a bulky package. Many of the patrons call one another by name and ask after the well-being of the family.

At the "service" counter, where you will have to stand in line, folks have zingers ready—stuff about the postal system ripping everyone off, spending all of its money on all of those "This Window Closed" placards instead of hiring enough help. Clerks like Larry and Gene are virtually immune to all of this—and always have something to say about how they enjoy taking your money anyway.

None of this is too serious. The same clerks who smugly peddle overpriced stamps will go to the trouble of handing you out a parcel that can't wait until Monday, even if it's a few minutes after closing time on Friday, or on Saturday morning, if you beat on the door and beg, or look through your lockbox to the back of the Post Office and holler. They'll even sometimes arrange for "emergency" duck stamps when you have last-minute hunters coming on Saturday, (it's already Friday evening, and none of the unexpected arrivals remembered to buy their stamps.) They do it not because they have to, but because this is small town, you're neighbors and everybody gets in a pickle once in a while.

We don't have to apologize for neighbors looking out for neighbors. If you're a really small town probably everybody's on the volunteer fire department, and more than a few are volunteer emergency medical personnel. You're too far from a "big city" to count on them for help.

Volunteers run the stock show, the Little League, Little Dribblers, flag football, 4-H, Boy Scouts, Girl Scouts, Campfire Girls, PTO at the schools, Red Cross, Hospital Auxiliary, Sheriff's Reserves, Friends of the Library and County Historical Association.

Don't apologize for knowing the local sheriff and his deputies, police chief, game warden, J.P., highway patrolmen, county judge, county commissioners, county clerk, tax assessor, district judge, school board, city commission, probably even the dog catcher—if there is one—by their first names. Local government and law enforcement work better serving known faces than strangers.

We shouldn't apologize for what is mostly low-key front-page news in the local paper, that we call our volunteer firemen/neighbors heroes when they rescue somebody from a burning building, or a couple of our hometown student nurses resuscitate a traffic accident victim and save their life.

It may be small town, but folks still get together to harvest a neighbor's crop when they are down with illness, to help with cleanup and get life going again after a fire or a weather disaster. I've seen folks come from miles away with their own tractors and equipment to help fight a grass fire or to save most of a wheat crop when a lightning strike touched off an inferno. Nobody told them to come, to bring tractors and plows and water tanks, to face risk. They just saw the smoke, knew what a neighbor stood to lose, and came hell-for-leather.

"Rush hour" in a small town lasts ten minutes. We won't apologize for that, nor for having dirt and grease under our fingernails; for being able to see spectacular risings and settings of the sun morning and evening; for being able to lie in the cool grass of the back yard of a summer evening and stare up at the stars; for witnessing nature's still-wild side that holds that some things must die that others may live, and that everything that we eat really doesn't just magically appear at the grocery.

Certainly, small town folk should make no apology for sharing their gardens, produce of their fruit trees, output of their kitchen ovens.

Neighbors give endlessly to untold good causes, bestowing time and talent and money.

I'm not sorry to live amidst small town atmosphere where you can walk up to someone's door and knock, or call them on the phone at night and get permission to hunt on their farm or ranch. All that neighbors of this sort require of you is that you look out for the livestock and irrigation equipment and close all of the gates behind you.

No apology needed for coming from places where we look out for and root for one another's kids all through school and keep up with them long after they've graduated.

Some folks are not too worldly or sophisticated. We are just small town.—Really can't say we're sorry.

The Folks Behind You

Graduating Seniors: Turn around and take a look at who's been behind you all the way.

To graduating high school seniors:
On commencement evening, following the processional to a piano or school band rendition of "Pomp and Circumstance," and once the class members have all been seated, I hope you'll turn around in your chair in the gymnasium, or the auditorium, or the football stadium at Hereford, or Friona, Farwell or Bovina or Lazbuddie, Vega or Adrian, and take a look behind you for a moment. In fact, I think that it would be a grand idea if the whole senior class would stand up together and turn around, so that you have a better view. You don't have to make a big deal out of it, just look a minute, and soak it all in.

Who do you see out there in the rows of theater seats, or in those "plush" folding metal chairs, or in the rarified air up there in the bleachers, probably fanning themselves and squirming and fidgeting?

Here's who I bet you don't find.—You won't see Dan Rather, or Tom Brokaw, or Peter Jennings, or talk show hosts—not even any of the celebrities from area television stations.

That's because the big-time media folks don't know you, and probably don't care to, unless you meet their news needs for the spectacular and the controversial and the violent. Face it kids, graduation in Adrian isn't big-time network stuff. Your winning of an academic or athletic or citizenship award doesn't qualify as important news to the world.

Look closely, though.—Right out there are folks it matters immensely to—Moms and Dads, grandparents, aunts and uncles, cousins and friends from school, preachers and teachers and coaches and business folks from your community. They are in their usual place, where they have been since the day you started kindergarten—behind you all the way.

You will never see a gathering of folks who care any more about you or want the best for and from you, who have been willing to sacrifice more so that you could achieve than those souls right out there.

These are the supporters who went to all your ball games and cheered you on from the time you were in Kids Inc. football, or Little Dribblers basketball, or YMCA sports. They drove the miles to your games—even if they were in Perryton or Paducah or in the sandy cotton country of the South Plains.

They hauled the team around to compete in tournaments, wore the road out going to junior high volleyball contests, and when the whirlwind of high school came, they would get you to a band contest and ferry you to the next event on the same Saturday, while you dressed in the back of the van on-the-go.

They beat tire grooves in the road to College Station in celebration of your success in qualifying for State 4-H Roundup year after year.

They followed you to band contests—even when the events were up in Borger and later, in Amarillo, where it was blowing snow. They sat in the stands and cheered your performance when the weather was so foul that even dogs and cats had the good sense to stay in.

They volunteered to run the concession stand at ball games, to serve as event judges at the school's big speech competitions, helped line up the props for UIL one-act play, hosted all-night slumber parties and when you were in dire straits, even attempted to help with homework problems.

They would sit through over an hour of proceedings just to see you handed a single subject award or a carnation recognizing you as a National Honor Society member.

They would discuss with you and really listen to how you felt about things, whenever and wherever you felt you needed to talk.

They did it all because they care about you, and it was their joy to, and they are looking for great things from you.

By the way, just because CBS, ABC, and NBC aren't around, don't think you've been ignored.

Out there in the audience you'll probably see familiar faces with notepads and cameras in their lap. The camera-bearing ones will probably be scurrying about, snapping pictures of you and your classmates.

That's because they are from your hometown paper, your local radio stations, and to them, you and your accomplishments ARE big news.

Nobody will ever champion your accomplishments and feature you more prominently in their pages and newscasts, or do a better job of reporting how you have succeeded than these folks do, because you are a hometown, country kid and they are proud of you.

Okay, better turn back around and get back to the ceremony at hand. You've still got that diploma to collect.

Just don't ever forget all of those folks sitting out there, who will always be "behind" you.

Catch You Next Time

Folks don't get treated like this just anywhere.

It's nice to run across folks who really do play fair.—I took my old pickup, the only vehicle that I ever bought brand-new, back in 1974, to Thad's magneto shop a while back. I have been driving the "red bomb" for a long time—so long that I am told that in only a couple more years I can register and tag it as an antique vehicle.

The red bomb has acquired honest wear and a few operating quirks. Weird things were happening with the electrical system when I called on Thad. The panel and interior lights worked only part of the time, if at all, the lighter socket wouldn't run my cellular phone, turn signals going goofy—that sort of stuff.

Not being keen on tracking down an electrical wiring problem by sorting through a color-coded maze and not at all confident in my ability to find a short if there was one somewhere, I opted to take my problem to a pro.

Thad and his boys, Randall and Nate, have been jockeying magnetos and alternators, generators and starters, and mazes of vehicular wiring for years. Debbie keeps the paperwork straight and checks up on them often enough to mostly keep them out of trouble. She has had enough experience teaching kindergarten that she can handle these guys.

You will see cop cars and ambulances at Thad's place pretty often, but it's because the cop house boys are there to get the overhead light systems on their patrol vehicles wired-up, not to raid the joint.

Thad sells "hot" batteries that are long-lived and will crank in the cold or the heat. He can work wonders with starters—even old worn-out 1974 Ford pickup starters. He doesn't often get his wires crossed. I guess you could call his shop a stronghold of consumer confidence.

When I brought my wayward pickup in, Thad played with the fuse box a little bit, clipped a couple of lights-and-whistles gadgets into it to test currents, pried out a fuse and worked the connectors inside the fuse box over with a small wire brush. He plugged the brushed-up fuse back where it went.—I have had nary a problem since.

Once the success of the treatment had been assessed, I figured it was pay-up time and peeled out my wallet. Thad waved me off. "No charge. Catch you next time."

Right across the street from Thad's is Mike's auto shop. There are enough vehicles-in-waiting parked in front of Mike's garage so that the place looks like a rent-a-wreck lot.

I've had my rigs at Mike's many times. Brakes and bearings, fuel pump, power steering pump, timing chain for a little Buick Skylark, radiator work, steering linkage, rack-and-pinion repair, all sorts of tuning and timing and belts and hoses and road-readiness checks and such. Mike is a throwback in certain respects. He stands behind his work.

Before I headed out on a long road trip in warm temperatures, I wanted to make sure that everything under the hood was up-to-snuff. The air conditioner had been squalling like a pining panther. I figured that there must be a bearing in there that was not long for this world.

Mike kept my rig for an afternoon. When I came by to pick it up, walking amidst the scattered tools and engine and transmission parts, my feet crunching in the texture of the oil-absorbing litter perpetually scattered on the floor, the old wagon hummed and the cooler didn't utter a squeak.

"How bad's the damage?" I reached for my checkbook to settle up.

Mike wiped the current layer from his greasy hands with a red rag that came from his hip pocket and smiled. "Aw, heck. All I did was tighten a couple of belts. No charge. I'll catch you next time."

On down the street to the west, not too much farther, Foy ran his Early Bird Shop for many years. He finally hung up his wrenches when the auto dealership next door got ambitious and thought they needed to expand and take up his little building.

My rigs made a few stops at the Early Bird, too. Mostly front-end and brake-related maladies. Last time that I was in, just before Foy retired, he practiced his art on some brake pads for the old red bomb.

We talked fishing, always an appropriate topic in Foy's shop, and we talked the impossibly high price of new vehicles, auto parts and dealership mechanic work.

Foy put the whoa back in my brakes. When tally-ho time came, the sum he figured up seemed impossibly modest.

"Aren't you selling yourself short," I asked.

Foy had an elbow on his knee, his foot propped on the bumper where it had acquired a slight bend in a too-close encounter with a fencepost.

"Naw, this will have you in good shape. You don't need to spend a bunch of money and all I need out of this is enough to buy fish bait. I'll catch you next time."

You don't get treated like this just anywhere.

I think that these hometown mechanics and magneto jockeys, all working within hollering distance of one another, have developed themselves quite a startling little business concept.—Treat folks right and they will keep coming back.—You'll always have the chance to catch them next time.

The "Old Cranks"

Remember the one about why a classroom is like a Model-T?

Insistent summons from jangling electronic bells decreed that we must move from the outdoors and into the confines of academia.

We shuffled down the long hallways pockmarked by classroom doors into a world of equal parts familiarity and mystery, answering, not with any great enthusiasm, the summons. Infernal metallic chimes chided us to take our places for this journey supposedly bound for learning.

Those to be indoctrinated with the stuff of knowledge flopped down at desks, nursing misgivings over a school year that had not only encroached upon, but had summarily executed summer. Freedom had been too swiftly lost.

Smells and sights of the place hit us full in the senses.

Floors fresh-waxed, desks polished, blackboards clean-washed, all sporting shines that would not last long.

Bulletin boards were brightly-decorated with messages and images that had been painstakingly and laboriously created through hours of effort.

Impossibly neat examples of printed or cursive lettering, depending upon your grade level, were displayed in spaces above the blackboards—lofty examples of what we were to set about emulating in the way of penmanship.

On the classroom air was the waxen bouquet of new boxes of Crayolas, still sharp-tipped and elongated, having not yet been dulled or broken by heavy-handed pressure in their work.

Bottles of white paste glue with brushes in the lid or rubber-tipped bottles of the syrup-colored kind had their own distinct odor.

New pencils with their cores of soft No. 2 lead awaited grinding to points of performance at the sharpener on the wall at the front of the classroom. The contraption had adjustable ports for accommodating several different sizes of pencils. The hand-turned sharpener reeked of wood and lead shavings.

Big Chief tablets with their pages of coarse newsprint and the familiar red, chief-adorned cover were for the lower-level grades. Spiral composition books and packets of blue-ruled notebook paper for the "upper classmen" were clean and new and uncreased, like mellow fields ready-to-plant.

The new paper was soon to be covered with our struggles at long division, fractions, algebraic ineptitude, spelling, sentence diagrams and essays. Smears and smudges would accompany the scrawlings, marking the places where our now-new green or tan or red-and-gray rubber-smelling erasers would be set to work at correction.

Through time, instruction, repetition and practice, all of these tools of our student trade were put to use. Somewhere in the mistake-laden process, and sometimes, in spite of ourselves, we fooled around and learned something.

I've sometimes had misgivings about school systems and whether-or-not today's are teaching our kids anything. I've also seen that there are still enough dedicated teachers who are more than willing to give the time and effort to meet our kids' needs.—There ought to be some learning going on.

If the kids—and their parents—have the desire to work toward learning and getting an education, the instruction and help is there.

A well-worn joke inhabits schoolhouses: Why is a classroom like a Model T?—Because there's an old crank up front and a bunch of little nuts inside.

Given the daunting challenges of modern teaching, it is amazing how few of those at the head of classrooms truly turn out to be "old cranks."

To be sure, there are some cranks and soreheads in the teaching ranks just like anywhere else, and they do damage. There are also a lot of fine and dedicated folks.

Some teachers like to get their "stern bluff" in early, in the first few days of school.

Those who come on as the most stern at the start of a school year sometimes turn out to be the best eggs, the instructors that kids learn the most from, and maybe even have fun doing it.

I admit, I don't understand what motivates folks to become teachers. How do they do it day-in and day-out? Surely it can't be the hours—or the pay.

Visiting with veteran teachers often reveals that they have harbored a lifelong desire to teach. This desire was frequently fired by one of their own teachers. These career-inspiring teachers set an example others sought to emulate.

Gifted teachers take great satisfaction in touching the lives of youngsters and work tirelessly toward this end. They delight in the growth and success of their students.

One of the teacher organizations used a slogan a few years ago about how "teachers touch lives."

It's true. A heavy-handed sort just putting in their time or drunk with the power of the position can do harm to a student's self-esteem. That sort of tragic damage can be hard to overcome, even by good teachers many years later.

Caring teachers guide, instruct, inspire—and prove a lifelong blessing—even if they *did* murder summer.

Soil Science 301

Students learned not only soil classification, but an appreciation for life's gifts.

Students, when they are lucky, run across a few truly inspiring teachers in the course of their high school and college academic careers.

For me, there were several at West Texas State University, including Kathleen Collins of the English department, whose creative writing classes fostered humility and inspiration, and Dr. Fred Rathjen of the History department, the superlative master of no-notes lecture and abiding appreciation for the intricacies of the Great Plains.

Knowledge-givers sometimes impart gems of wisdom and insight in the course of their contact with students.

Our daughter, Jaime, has been fortunate throughout her academic career in encountering instructors of this ilk.

One of her favorites has been Dr. Murray Milford, who was serving as interim dean of the Department of Agronomy and Soil Science 301 professor at Texas A&M University at the time of his retirement from the classroom.

I knew we were onto something when, in one of her calls home, Jaime asked that I ship to her in College Station not money, clothing, or some forgotten item, but a can of "earth from her home country" to be utilized in her Soil Science lab.

I gathered a good sample on one of my subsequent trips to a local farm, packaged it up tightly and placed the canister of earth with a note in the mailing box. I told Jaime, the best that I could, that the contents here were not just dirt—but represented a tiny sampling of the thin layer of topsoil that holds the world together and feeds us all—the substance of life-support itself.

In my years of working with agriculture and wildlife, I had tried to instill some appreciation for the land and natural resources in her. While she was enrolled in Soil Science 301 I noticed Jaime speaking eloquently about the goodness of the soil and growing food and poking around more at growing things.

Dr. Milford endeared himself to our student not so much for his grasp of soil science, classification and stewardship of resources, but for his understanding of and appreciation for human nature and the important things of everyday life.

Jaime loved Dr. Milford's Soil Science class. During the semester that she took the course and an associated lab, she spoke often of Dr. Milford's wise observations in her frequent calls home.

Even after she had completed the course, Jaime returned to Dr. Milford's classroom to sit in on his final lecture before retirement.

Dr. Milford's teachings on soil properties were excellent, I'm sure, but that wasn't what Jaime valued most, came back as a visitor to hear and to vividly recall.

Rather, it was Dr. Milford's comments on the way things are in the world that stuck with her and gave her a renewed sense of appreciation for opportunities—shared by parents, incidentally.

In his final lecture, Dr. Milford threw out to his class and assorted guests a number of thought-provoking statistics:

* Only 60 percent of the world's populace has access to clean water.

* Nearly 60 percent of the world's populace is malnourished.

* Just 30 percent of the world's population has been taught to read.

* Only **one percent** of the total population of Earth has the opportunity to go to college.

That last statistic can be taken as an especially poignant reminder to the masses of young American men and women situated on college campuses all across this country.

Higher education, it would seem, is one of those abundant blessings we so easily take for granted here in this country. We have to stop sometimes and remind ourselves just how fortunate we are.

The invaluable lessons that Jaime was able to glean from Dr. Milford's Soil Science classes didn't particularly center around Pullman and Olton clay loams, although caring for the good earth was certainly stressed.

Important lessons one Aggie soil science professor taught our daughter and legions of students that passed through his classroom during a distinguished career plowed the fertile fields of honesty, compassion, perseverance, reflection and graciousness.

Those students who sank roots deep into Dr. Milford's rich seedbed of knowledge harvested a bumper crop from this portion of their college experience.

Ten-Speed and Tylenol

Pedaling with my riding companion on a summer evening, I find that we have made a circle.

A pleasant late-summer evening had beckoned us to mount up and ride.

My bicycling companion, seated on a 10-speed, was cruising along effortlessly on the other side of the street with long, smooth rotations of the legs and knees. She periodically selected gear settings that would offer greater resistance and give her a better "workout."

Running well off the pace and already feeling "worked-over," I pumped frantically on my red Western Auto "one-speed," a machine deserving of the operating slogan: No gears—just guts.

Feeling their wobble and clunk, I hoped that the age-worn and often-aired tires would hold up.

Though my legs were tight and the muscles already complaining, I strived not to grimace with the effort required to buck the mild breeze that was freshening at the fall of night.

Gut-it-up I told myself, not wanting to wimp out as a gaunt and grim-faced slacker when my fellow rider looked radiant, totally fit and relaxed.

We made the first turn less than a half-mile from the house. There was lots of pedaling ahead before we completed the circuit.

Eventually the clunking tires seemed to round themselves out, my pedaling became, if not rhythmic, at least more even-paced, and frankly, the pacesetter probably eased up a bit. I settled in behind her lead and kept the red bike rolling.

Panting less and wheeling a little more easily through residential streets, I got to thinking on times past when the rapid-rolling ten-speed pilot over there was a Munchkin riding strapped in a "tailgunner" seat over the back fender of the very same red one-speed that was challenging me now.

Didn't seem all that many years ago when most every summer and fall evening, we would load up and go in search of pedal-powered adventure to the tune of gravel crunching and asphalt humming against the tires.

Meandering through streets, taking our shortcuts as we needed them, we established familiar routes where we would meet friendly folk out for an evening stroll. Down one street we often encountered the nice people who had sold us this Munchkin's baby bed. They always wanted to talk a bit to the passenger in the tailgunner seat. Over the varying routes, there were smiles and waves and howdies from walkers and porch-sitters and yard-tenders, amidst chances to dodge sprinkler streams splashing in the street. We saw, petted and were accompanied by many friendly dogs—and one sort-of grumpy big one we thought was going to swallow us bicycle and all. Thank goodness, he backed off.

Different days we took different routes—up by the baseball field to watch the boys and girls at play, down the quiet residential stretch past the place where the man constantly hoed the long rows of his huge garden, up past the Allsup's or the Dairy Queen, where nourishment for furthering the journey could be obtained.

With fall, the drum cadences and horn overtures of the Mighty Maroon band wafted through the evening air to be plainly heard in our front yard. Our journeys naturally gravitated to the source of the sound—the band practice field over at the high school. Those evenings were electrified by the sounds and scenery of the band marching and playing, the thumping of the drums serving to rev-up excitement in the passenger for the day she would be in the band.

The passenger eventually outgrew her over-the-fender seat. The time came for a bicycle just her size. Wobbly learning, graduation from training wheels and the journeys continued, the big red bike in the lead, the pink and green one following.

"Not so fast, Daddy, wait up. My legs are tired." I would ease back to slow, lazy revolutions of the pedals.

The riding partner's bike got bigger, the pace quickened. There were races, including a spectacular Dad wreck that fortunately, hurt nothing but the remote for the garage door opener.

Busy high school days, kid at college. Bicycles too long in the shed, until a summer evening.

"Dad, can you air up my bicycle so I can go riding?"

Plug in the air compressor, blast off the grit of time, firm up the tires on the 10-speed and might as well get the red bike out and see if the tires will hold.

Now, here we are, wheeling in the summer breeze, kid in the lead, me following, knees sore, think I'll need Tylenol when we get home, but feeling pretty good about the ride.

We roll up to Centre Street and pause, standing astride our bikes.

"Want to turn for home now, Dad, or do you want to ride a little longer?"

Legs stiff, knees sore. I wouldn't mind riding a little longer, I allow, but I have to add:

"Not so fast, Jaime. Wait up, my legs are tired."

Danger: College Move-In

Hazards far greater than moving 500-pound beds face Dads during this job.

Parents are just calming down from their euphoric outbursts of celebration over their kids finally getting through high school and across the stage at commencement with diploma in hand when the next challenge comes along.

Some parents probably found the end-of-May gatherings in gymnasiums and auditoriums and on football fields real nail-biters—evidently expecting some school administrator to suddenly come to their senses during commencement, leap from their chair, shout out loud that it was all a big mistake, and jerk the freshly-awarded diplomas from the clutches of wanna-be graduates.

Easy, now. The kids have their diplomas, the mortarboards have been tossed and the high schools aren't going to declare it all a bad joke and call the kids back.

Having survived high school, would it be construed as cruel to mention at this point that one of the sternest tests of the parent/young adult relationship still lies ahead?

This is only fair warning for those who will be transplanting their kid bag and baggage to some far-off campus in August.

Be petrified, parents. What lies ahead is that onerous ordeal known as MOVING THE KID IN AT COLLEGE!

Moving in at college can prove—how shall we put this—less than relaxing.

Small wonder. College move-in occurs in the presence of a volatile mixture of characters, circumstances and attitudes. Start with highly-independent thinking young adults out to launch their new life, add parents set-in-their-ways who are out to prove they are **not** dinosaurs, and add a physically demanding and highly emotional set of circumstances involving a major life change.

It's bad enough that all of these ingredients are combined, but invariably, kids arrive on campus amidst the very hottest days of August.

You've heard of sweat equity? Move-in at college is a big down payment that doesn't get you one cent of credit against tuition or room and board expenses, unfortunately.

Parents and student make a grueling drive to big campus and prepare to colonize.

Parking? What parking? The campus may cover 1,000 acres, but spaces for conveniently positioning your vehicle in order to unload at dormitories are about as available as tenured professorships—and jealously guarded by campus cops who giddily fill their ticket-writing quotas on the naive greenhorns-on-campus.

You must leave your vehicle a minimum of a half-mile from the dormitory where your new freshman will be living.

The vehicles in your entourage are laden with every worldly possession of the child—including one entire closet full of clothing, wall decorations, posters, several highly-breakable items including mirrors, plus the kitchen sink, microwave oven/refrigerator, and at least seventeen large items you can't imagine they will ever need.

Perhaps you remembered to bring along a dolly or a red wagon or some sort of freight transfer device that you can load down. As you trundle across campus, looking like something out of the Grapes of Wrath, you spill contents intermittently at assorted curbs and cracks in the sidewalk and pause to pick them up and re-stack to the tune of admonitions to "Be careful, Dad."

During your seventh such journey, you are growing accustomed to seeing the constant stream of beds and bookcases and television sets and computers being toted across campus by students and parents. Still, you are astonished to witness two hefty college boys toting a full-size sofa over this half-mile course, effortlessly holding the thing over their heads and happily plodding along. What is even more astonishing is the thought of actually fitting that couch into a sardine can of a dormitory room.

Arriving with another load at the aforementioned closet-sized dorm room you find it is now jammed with the flotsam of move-in. The moving-in process is not flowing smoothly. Everywhere are yet-to-be emptied boxes, pillows and linens and computers and monitors, room decorations and piles of clothing.

"Where are you going to put all of this stuff?"

Your perfectly innocent question evokes withering glances from wife and daughter, who are arguing about how the beds should be placed. Daughter wants her bed angled in a space-consuming manner. Mom is insisting on a more space-sensible arrangement against the wall. Dad can keep his opinion to himself, thanks.

At the height of the debate, the new roommate arrives, compounding the congestion, but at last resolving the issue of where the beds will go. The sweating father is directed to move the boxy bookcase bed and mattress against the wall opposite of where it is currently sitting.

Said bed weighs at least 500 pounds. With groaning, grunting and muttering under his breath, fast-diminishing Dad manages to slide the bed into its new position, then leaves the room fast, figuring correctly that he is in much less danger of injury going after another load on the dolly than sticking around here.

This is how college move-in goes. Somehow, despite all of the jangled nerves and strong opinions, all of the stuff gets sorted out and, with any luck, nobody gets hurt permanently.

When, mercifully, the job is finished and it's time for Mom and Dad to head home, tears and tension are shed. Hopefully, by the end of the ordeal, the kid is safely situated and you can laugh at the ridiculousness of it all.

Endings and Beginnings

It is the way of things in the small-town farm country
to celebrate life in coming together
to lay one passed-on in the good earth.

It's easy to visualize him in khakis smelling slightly of gasoline or diesel, a little washed-at-and-missed grease on his hands, an ear-flapped cap on his head in cold weather and a mischievous smirk on his face as he "worked over" kids in his lap with thorough, tickling demonstrations of "how a horse bites." He was a prankster, comedian and practical joker through much of his life. Though his Christian name was Louis Joseph, everybody knew him as "Bud."

He amused nieces, nephews and daughters by drawing funny-looking faces that he called "hootenannies." These were rendered with quick strokes of his Eversharp pencil on notebooks he kept in a shirt pocket. He was almost always good for a soda pop down at Hart's four-star Green Frog Cafe and it seemed that no matter who was sitting in the place, they always knew him.

For many years Bud was associated with mysterious appearances of Santa Claus at schools, businesses and homes in Hart and Nazareth. Funny how he would vanish about the time the man in red showed up.

Through his work in church organizations, on behalf of veterans, and as a member of the American Legion, he came to know a lot of folks. He liked baseball, especially "Legion ball."

Bud's family and ours have lived and grown in a middle ground, four miles from Hart, eight miles from Nazareth. The Steiert clan has belonged in some capacities to both communities through the years and perhaps we have realized something of the best of both.

Fierce rivals in high school football and basketball, one community almost exclusively Catholic, the other both Protestant and Catholic, Nazareth and Hart have had their differences. Some of these have become more vague over the years. Maybe we have all done some growing up.

Despite differences, the communities can come together on important things that really matter. Neither has ever gotten so pretentious that it doesn't pretty-much shut down during a native's funeral.

This isn't get-rich-quick country—never has been as material things go. The only oil money you see around here is that handed over to pay for a few cases of 30 or 40-weight, or a tankful of gas down at Jim Black's Oil Company or Butch Martinez's station in Hart, or at Kleman's Nazareth Oil and Gas, where the coffee crowd gathered early of the mornings to resolve the world's problems.

Growing corn, milo, wheat and cotton at Hart or Nazareth won't put you in a higher tax bracket. Riches more lasting can be had out here in the small town farm country—growing good kids, an environment that nurtures body and soul, neighbors, the sense of continuity from way back in aught-when to now.

Bud's funeral was a chapter in an ongoing story that moves families and neighbors from two communities built on pioneering spirit, only a dozen miles apart, to come together. This chapter was played out in a familiar church and cemetery in Nazareth. Standing together in the church and the tidy, peaceful little cemetery behind it were representatives of generations neighbors who grew up taking sustenance from the land here, and from one another.

At the funeral procession an American Legion honor guard of farm boys spanning generations formed-up in salute. The stars and stripes and the blue-and-gold Legion flags were borne by World War II vet Alvin Anderle, now passed on himself, and Julius Birkenfeld, a Vietnam era vet.

Standing at attention and looking smart, yet suitably plain in their dark "overseas caps" and white shirts, were country boys who left the home fields for stints of duty in the World War II, Korea, and Vietnam eras. They were farm boys we knew—"Junior" Hochstein, a goose hunting and Legioning pal of Bud's who harvested my Dad's cotton crop many times; good-natured and funny Bob Schulte, a years-ago classmate who once left a cleat mark across my chest when I clipped him stealing second base in a schoolyard baseball game; others of the Schulte clan, Elmer, and Clyde, a classmate of my older sister who married Lisa Lacy, a neighbor girl from just down the road; Tom Hoelting, a parts man we watched grow up only a couple miles from our home ground; James Wilhelm, from the dryland country near the draw north of Nazareth where rains are rare and appreciated; Art Brockman, brother of Joyce, who was a classmate for nine years; and Clyde Birkenfeld, bugler, and brother to Darlene, another classmate.

These guys carried on just one more muster in their small but active Legion post's long-running legacy of remembering farm village boys who served with honor, of calling to mind where life is centered, where the heartland lies—the meaning of service for God and country.

They took the time, though their farms and fields and businesses needed attention, to pay tribute to one of their own. The folding and presentation of the colors, the crashing of rifle volleys against the peaceful morning, the soul-piercing notes of Taps—played three times, as, in a community tradition, the bugler turned so that the notes carried to every corner of the village so that all would hear—bore added meaning coming from home folk.

Neighbors gathered from two towns, farmers and stockmen, truckers and welders, laborers and storekeepers. Folks who had neighbored, harnessed the horses and mules and hitched the buggies, stacked the bundles, spilled the paint, pulled the pranks and never ratted, walked the miles to school together, sweated-out the crops, reaped the harvests of delight and despair, shared the long windies and the laughter with Bud and Dad, Tony and Mary and Ann. They gave the comfort they could through simple acts of consideration, preparing food, sharing stories, being there.

That is how the cycle of the small town farm country goes. The rural folk celebrate your beginnings, work and laugh and cry and sometimes argue and even fight with you through the years, and at one ending and a new beginning, they come together to lay you in the good earth from whence all things come.

The Lord in His infinite wisdom plunked small towns down in farm country.

No matter where circumstances may take you or how far you move away, it seems the circle of small town farm country neighbors can always open to encompass you.

Great Horny Toads

A whole generation of kids grew up toting these mini-dinosaurs in their jean pockets.

The resumption of school seems always to call to mind initial encounters with the public education system back in the late 1950's. In that era terrified first graders (at least I was terrified) at Nazareth got their start in what was essentially a one-room schoolhouse—if you don't count the coat closets and the restrooms attached at the back of the building. The first grade building was separated from the rest of the school by roughly a city block, meaning a nice brisk walk to the school lunchroom across town every day. The first grade building was adjacent to the church, and not much of a stretch of the legs from the cemetery.

There was a big moonscape sort of yard, much-cratered, mostly devoid of grass, where the whole pack of youngsters was turned out for recess. We were summoned back to the classroom by a big handbell that we got to ring in turns.

Among the games on the playground were baseball, jumping rope, tag and swinging from the pipe fence around the school yard and cemetery. If these were not satisfactory, a chief playground amusement was observation, pursuit and handling of "horny toads," fat and abundant on this vast playground. The rough-and-tumble schoolyard included many red ant beds, and large live ants are a mainstay horny toad food.

The correct name for these amusing reptiles is *horned lizard*. They are not a toad or frog at all, but it wouldn't sound nearly as amusing in Bugs Bunny cartoons if a flustered Yosemite Sam hollered "great horned lizards."

A whole generation of Texas Panhandle kids grew up playing with and carrying "horny toads" in their jean pockets. This fond title for the prehistoric-looking little lizards is hard to shake.

I'm not sure what it was about horny toads that attracted kids to them—maybe the same thing that forever compels elementary schoolers to dote on dinosaurs. Not even the squealing girls or the teacher minded having a horny toad shoved in their faces all that much—if they weren't too big. Boys and girls caught them in droves to handle and pet and watch and release again. It was such a contrast to run your fingers over their rough, spiny backs and that fearsome, horned head, then turn them over in your palm and rub the smooth underbelly as they closed their eyes.

We caught mostly little ones, but sometimes would corner a real trophy, five inches or longer, fatly round and low-slung to the ground, horned head up and pivoting as it reared-up on its forelegs to make itself look larger and more threatening.

In all of the horny toad catching and handling that we did, I don't recall ever seeing one demonstrate a defensive tactic that naturalists say they possess. When alarmed, horned lizards can squirt blood from their eyes for a distance of several feet—with no apparent harm to themselves. This is something that would surely have set off wild reaction on the part of a pack of curious first graders. Blood squirting from the eyes is thought to be a means of deterring small mammals that bother the lizards—I guess annoyingly inquisitive first graders weren't deemed by the horny toads as sufficiently threatening to justify their staging such a dramatic display.

The little reptiles bury themselves in loose sand or soil to regulate body temperature and to escape predators. In the fall, horny toads bury up and go into hibernation, to emerge again in April or May—just in time for the first grade playground crowd to get in a little more action with them before the end of the school year.

We wondered at the ability of horny toads to wander among the fiercely stinging red ants with relative impunity. I guess their spiny coat was pretty good armor. We usually turned them loose in close proximity to plenty of this crawly food and appreciated their doing-in the ants that sometimes caused us misery.

Sadly, the number of horny toads has declined sharply since those days. They are now on the state's threatened species list and there are research efforts underway to document just why. Widespread use of pesticides and altering of habitat are thought to be primary reasons. A horny toad has to consume a lot of ants since they are of relatively low nutritional value. Some biologists think that the invasion of the imported fire ant in Texas may be partly responsible for the horny toad's decline. Fire ants, aggressive and deadly, force out other larger, less aggressive ants. Efforts to eradicate fire ants also eliminate the native ants horny toads relish, leaving them without a suitable food source.

We still see a few horny toads in this part of the state and they are yet relatively common in the Rolling Plains' rough country.

Thinking on initial school days, we can still call back a lot of the fixtures. The classroom, with its examples of properly hand-printed letters on cards above the blackboards, Big Chief tablets and huge pencils to fit small hands, Crayolas, paste that kids sometimes ate, blunt-nosed scissors, big desks with folding seats and our names beautifully printed on cards on the corner of these, Dick and Jane readers, spelling books, cross-country walks to the lunchroom, afternoon milk breaks, girls skipping rope, recess and clanging handbells, and those prickly pocket pals, great horny toads.

Goose Tales

Geese display more sense than lots of people.

It is the rare farmstead now that has a pond and a scattering of barnyard geese and ducks. That is part of hurry-up, prepackaged living, I guess. Nobody has time to mess with farmyard critters these days.

When I was a boy we had a pond on either side of the house, a yard full of noisy geese, green-headed ducks and speckled guineas, and a source of amusement close at hand. It was fun watching the ducks and geese cruising placidly on the ponds, dipping up for goodies on the bottom, waddling along on parade from one waterhole to the other.

One old gander was in love with the orange Case tractor that we used to plow wheat stubble. He would buddy-up to the tractor every day during the noon hour, gabbling contentedly while standing beneath the rig.

A close encounter could ensue when Dad tried to take the tractor back to the field after dinner. The gander was a jealous guardian of his prize tractor and was likely to hiss a challenge and even to give chase and attempt to pinch a plug out of the unwary.

Dad figured out the charm that the Case held for the gander. The tractor's drawbar brushed against the wheat stubble while plowing. The metal was polished to a mirrorlike finish. Apparently, the gander could see his reflection in the shiny drawbar. He was taken with the handsome honker he saw there and reluctant to part company.

A gray gander took a shine to Dad's blue GMC pickup and looked to go with it anytime it left the place. The gander would waddle frantically alongside the pickup as it pulled out of the driveway. With hectic honking and beating of wings the gander would lift into flight alongside the pickup. Sometimes the gander would stay with the pickup for the whole of the three-quarter mile drive to the highway before turning back for home.

One gusty day the gray gander didn't allow for one of the guy wires stabilizing the television antenna as he began his pickup-escorting flight. An unfortunate midair collision with the guy wire skinned him severely from head to tail. The gander survived, but his flying days were over. Afterward, he could only waddle in overdrive and scream his protest whenever the pickup departed.

We had a few of those knob-nosed Chinese geese. They were

handsomely streamlined birds, except for those bulbous knobs on their bills. I much preferred the smooth-faced gray-colored geese for looks. We raised one of the knob-nosers from a gosling, in company with a bunch of rooster chicks, since he was an abandoned orphan. That gander earned the name "Whittle-Whittle"—after his peculiar call. He taught the baby chicks to drink water. He couldn't take more than a couple of mouthfuls of feed without going to the waterer. The roosters embarrassed W.W. no end when they began to crow and he could not. Nor could the chickens relate to W.W.'s peculiar desire to be in water.—Doubtless, he had the last laugh. All of his classmates went to the frying pan. W.W. had the run of the place for years until coyotes came calling one night.

Tales of barnyard geese would not be complete in this part of the world without mention of the late and legendary Edwin "Goose" Ramey. Goose, a Castro County farmer and rancher, was an esteemed expert on geese. Folks were open-minded enough that they did not hold it against Goose that he also associated with the late Tom Draper—a legendary cat and coon hunter in his own right. Goose farmed between Dimmitt and Nazareth and saw his first wild geese in Castro County in 1913. He winged a Canada goose that year, brought it home, and nursed it until it could fly again. That goose took up residence at his farm and eventually mated with a domestic goose, producing offspring that were excellent flyers, but sterile. Ramey called them "mule geese."

For about 60 years Goose made his farm a convalescent center for wounded geese and banded many of the Canada geese that came to his farm. He kept wounded geese penned just long enough to heal, then set them free.

"The Old Man" was one of the wounded Canada ganders that Goose patched up and banded. That honker repaid Ramey's efforts by returning to his farm for 23 consecutive years.

One of Goose's "mule geese" was a big fellow dubbed "Buddy." This mule goose followed Ramey with doglike devotion, flying alongside his car or pickup. Ramey checked the flight speed of Buddy against his vehicle's speedometer. The goose could cruise at a steady 60 miles-per-hour and could make 80 and 90 mile-an-hour speeds for short intervals.

Ramey kept trying for 17 years before he succeeded in mating wild geese at his farm. He maintained ponds for the geese for many years.

With his trademark gravelly voice, Goose became a popular speaker on the ways of geese and weather. He had earned his moniker honestly by the time that it was attached, about 1926.

You'll hear remarks sometimes about somebody down the way not having "the sense God gave a goose."

Geese mate for life. The goose and gander share responsibilities on the nest and in seeing after the goslings. They are fierce defenders of their family but gregarious with and proud of their own. Make-do sorts, they happily hustle up a living just waddling around the farm and grazing weeds and shoots and odd bits of grain.

This credits geese, and deservedly so, with a fair amount of sense—certainly more than a lot of people show.

Beadie, the Goose Hunter

He may not see the flights
working above him with his eyes,
but he surely sees them with his heart.
He has become an *aficionado*.

If you are a wildfowler, January is a month to sit and suffer misery in the cold and, if you are lucky, to lure to a decoy spread and bring to bag the wild goose and the sharp-eyed sandhill crane.

Somewhere in the years since I moved to Hereford in the mid 1970's, I have come to be known as a goose hunter. Whether this reputation is deserved is a matter of debate. Evidently, folks thought I spent enough time trying that I must have become one.

In the country where I grew up, it was a big deal to bag a goose. Opportunity didn't present itself often. When it did, a lot of Texas low-crawling was generally called for to get close enough for a shot with the scattergun.

Some of the old timers used to say that if you bagged a goose once in seven years, you were doing pretty well.

Back about the 1970's, we began to see geese where they had previously been rare. Maybe they came with the shift to more corn production on the home grounds. Geese go through corn like—well—like corn goes through a goose.

My senior year in college, I had the good luck to decoy in two flights of geese with some homemade silhouette decoys while I was duck hunting and bagged a limit. This was an incredible feat for the Hart country back then.

Not until I came to Hereford did I begin to see flights of geese at regular intervals. I picked up the fine art of luring flocks to spreads of decoys with some degree of regularity and I learned to help my chances with calling.

I've shared a goose spread with a good many colorful and interesting characters and have been thoroughly indoctrinated in Humility 101, courtesy of the birds.

An enjoyable part of the grand sport has been the opportunity to help a number of women and youngsters to bag their first goose.

One of the most satisfying outings I've had would probably be the "first goose" experience for Beadie Brown, one of the Pied Pipers from down Hamlin-way. My friend, Beadie, is a man of rare vision—though he lost his eyesight as a child.

The fire of the hunter burns in Beadie—not blood lust—just respect for and curiosity about the game and its ways.

Beadie called me, out of the blue, several years ago about a goose hunt. In the first minute I talked with him long-distance on the phone, I liked him.

Beadie explained right-off that he was blind. Said he had never been on a goose hunt, didn't have a clue what it encompassed, but doggone, he sure would like to sit under a close-in flock of geese on the wing and just feel what it was like. He had a brother, Lance, who would bring him up if I would take them. I appreciated his enthusiasm and I told those Brown boys to just come ahead.

We got a great January morning for our hunt, toe-numbing cold, some low clouds and enough wind to keep the geese down. I had been lucky enough to find a "hot" plowed corn field that the birds really wanted into.

The Canadas worked for us that morning and Lance, Rick, George and I bagged several, taking our shots when their wings were set and their feet down.

Beadie was getting the feel of it all when a flock of snow geese, those awesomely wary packages of frustration-wrapped-in-feathers, did me a kindness.

Twenty-five or thirty of them came in high and whiffled, spilling altitude in great leaflike plunges, plummeting down in their haste to get to the corn field where we waited. Beadie, in camouflage, was lying next to me. I explained to him, the best I could, how those white geese were bombing in.

We let them come. I coaxed them with shrill yelps on my call, mimicking their doglike yammering. I had been telling Beadie all morning that snow geese were impossible to decoy, but here these came, as if they were on a mission.—I believe they were.

The snows skimmed right in on top of us, locked their wings, dropped their pinkish feet and back-pedaled not 10 feet above Beadie. He could hear the rush of wind through their primaries, feel the puffs of air from their fanning wings and he experienced the screeching clamor of the black wing-tipped birds. He kept moving his smiling face toward the commotion.

The snows slid off to one side of the spread, guns came up and six geese tumbled out of the flock.

I walked out and gathered a mature lesser snow, all pure white body and black wingtips, brought it back and plopped it in Beadie's lap. The flight of snows had given him the gift of a pass so close that the wind whistled in their wings. Another of the hunters, George, an artist from Rhode Island, pulled up a seat in the dirt next to Beadie and added to the magic moment.

A carver of wildfowl replicas, George explained goose anatomy well. He took hold of the fallen snow goose with one hand, took Beadie's hand in the other, and helped Beadie to trace the form and function of a goose, from wing primaries to tail feathers. Beadie soaked it all up. The smile was even broader.

That was a rare morning, those years ago, when the geese gifted us with a pass so close that *every* man could see.

Beadie and Lance come back to hunt geese with me sometimes. My friend, Beadie, has learned to talk goose through wood and plastic. He can lure them close with his own breath and has become an *aficionado* of the quest for the wild goose.

Beadie may not see all of the flocks working above the spread with his eyes, but he surely sees them with his heart.

Horse Sense, Dogies, and Belonging to Dogs

Animals can take amazing delight in sensibly doing their job. Quirks of fate sometimes let lucky people belong to a good horse or a decent dog.

Some animals have amazing talent. Dad bought an old mare for my younger sister. The mare had great "horse sense."

I don't know how old the mare was, but she had already experienced a long and illustrious career before she came to our place to stand in the fence corners and burn hay.

The late Clif Henderson, the tall, thin fellow that Dad horse-traded her from, told us that the mare had once been rodeo bucking stock. You would not have thought it, based on her mild disposition or her slow pace.

The mare mothered the dogie heifer calf that we kept in the corral with her. One time the calf got out and wandered into a nearby wheat field. I saddled the old horse and went after the dogie. There was no need to direct the mare. She went up to the calf, shoved it along with her chest and hustled it all the way back to the pen.

Any time my sister took the horse out for a ride, the dogie calf would stand at the fence and bawl. Her mama had up and left her.

The mare was infinitely patient with hair braidings and brushings and such.

One time Sis was giving a couple of the nieces a ride, leading the mare around with only a blanket on her back. The blanket took an unfortunate shift and the two kids came plummeting down hard. The instant the mare felt the load of youngsters shift from her back, she stopped cold—didn't even put her lifted foot down, lest she step on somebody.—An awful lot of presence of mind for an old rodeo horse. Thanks to "horse sense," the worst thing that happened to the nieces was the wind was knocked from them. With some coaxing, they eventually got back on the horse.

The mare often stood nose-to-nose in the corner of the corral, visiting with the resident farm dog.

It was not unusual to see my sister and the nieces, dog and mare, all sharing watermelon.

Some horses can certainly be dangerous, but there are some of them possessed of good nature and good sense, too.

Through quirks of fate, people sometimes are lucky and end up belonging to a decent dog—maybe more than one, if you are luckier than a puppy dog with two tails.

Some of these dogs may work stock, some will stay with you in the field, trotting alongside the tractor back-and-forth. Some are hunting companions or ride-around-in-the-pickup pals.

I have gotten to run with a few hunting dogs employed by folks who comprehend that their four-footed friends know way more than people do about the functions they are supposed to perform.

One of the first things in being successful with a dog is being smart enough not to mess them up. Just give them a general idea of what you want them to do and dog instinct takes care of most of the rest.

It's a rare pleasure afield to get to hunt with a dog whose greatest joy in life is to do, with enthusiasm, what you are asking of him.—*Birds in here, let's get 'em up—pant, pant, slobber, slobber—Kinda' sloppy shootin'—I'll just go fetch back that one ya' sailed off out there, boss.*

After we had a couple of gooseless hunts, I swear old chocolate-colored Tucker would positively skip and hop all the way out and back when he finally got to fetch a honker that we had knocked down. He sported a big, slap-happy Labrador grin all of the time. Tucker and his yellow running buddy, Molly, would argue over who got to fetch the bird. They were both gung-ho, can-do.

Their son, Beau, is quite a black beast in his own right—all enthusiasm and slap-happy silliness and demolition machine. He and I have come a ways in learning to work with each other. At just seven months, he wasn't half bad at fetching pheasants, even came up with a cockbird that three senior dogs couldn't find. I had a hard time faulting him the morning that I sent him to flush a rooster in front of us and he instead wheeled hard and went straight for a bird somebody had sailed that we were going to try and pick up on the walk back. He didn't return immediately when I called him back. I had marked that sailer and it was probably half-a-mile distant. Beau quickly lost his line on the bird. Once he did, he dropped his head and came sidling back to me. Though he had committed a breach of etiquette, it was hard to be mad at him for doing what was probably the right thing. I snapped on his leash, we took a line toward the bird and in a few minutes, Beau was lugging back that sailer. Like

I say, it's hard to fault a Lab for want-to.

Guess that's why the whole group of pheasant hunters I was walking with got such a laugh out of one of Beau's retrieves.

We were getting into the home stretch on a pass through a sorghum stubble field when a pair of roosters flushed. One thundered away in a hard right. Beau watched that bird, saw another Lab go rushing to retrieve it and politely stood where he was. He didn't see the second rooster that roared off almost straight away and was dropped nearly simultaneously. That bird was plenty close for Beau to retrieve, but he didn't budge.

I gave him a tweet on the whistle, he turned to take my direction and I pointed toward the area where the rooster had fallen, hollering, "Fetch!"

Beau looked around for a couple of seconds, then, without missing a beat, went racing the remaining length of the field to my pickup, down at the turnrow.

He leaped in the back of the pickup, rummaged around and shortly came galloping back to me, carrying a rooster he had retrieved from the pickup bed where I had left it after the previous up-and-back in the maize field.

I had told him to fetch, but hadn't specified which bird. Aiming to please, he made sure he brought me back a pheasant!

Experts say dogs don't necessarily understand emotions or human words.—I'm not so sure.

Another time when we were pheasant hunting, Beau was working a multiple drop of birds by the hunting party. He retrieved a very-much-still-alive rooster. In a hurry, he didn't quite place it in my hand before he turned to make the next retrieve and I missed getting hold of the bird.

The broken-winged rooster hit the ground running, sprinting away down a water furrow in the maize.

With the dog busy, I gave chase, puffing like a steam engine running hard after the fleeing pheasant.

Just as I was getting close enough to grab the on-the-lam rooster, a maize stalk jobbed firmly into the laces of my right boot and I went down like falling timber, essentially plowing a furrow with my nose.

Beau saw me go down, let out a yowl, then galloped the length of the field, yelping pitifully the whole way until he got to me.

I got up on my knees and the black dog poked his face in mine, still yelping. He licked me in the face, he circled around my legs as I stood up, he rubbed against my legs, all while still crying. Finally, I got back down, gathered him up in my arms and assured him I was okay. Once I told him I was okay, he was too. Certain that I was fine, he loped off, grabbed the escaping pheasant, brought it right to my hand and we rejoined the hunt... In that instant I understood that even if nobody else did, my dog thought a lot of me.

Pretty amazing, what a dog will put up with from us people and still idolize us. They don't care if we're handsome or homely, tall or short, rich or poor, cranky or less cranky. Their greatest pleasures are working for us and keeping our company. Given the people some dogs have to associate with, they work pretty cheap.

After a hard morning of hunting, a dog is certainly within his rights to park squarely in front of you when you break for a sandwich and give you accusing looks.

You know, I was the one that ran down that crippled pheasant, and I went on that 200- yard swim to gather in that wing-tipped mallard, and I hauled back that 12-pound Canada goose. All you did was shoot— and if you had done that less poorly, I wouldn't have had to go so far to get your birds. I deserve at least half of your sandwich, probably more.

There is no arguing with that look—the dog is right and deservedly, shares my lunch every time.

Yep, you're mighty lucky when you get to belong to a decent dog.

Politics Goes To the Dogs

**Every decent politician knows:
The first rule is you have to look out for *Numero Uno*.**

Maybe it's just me. Have you noticed that there is a lot of negative campaigning, and politics in general has gone to the dogs?

Herman was a hard-working decent sort: Took care of his family, paid his bills on time—installment payments on the big ones like the pickup and the house—helped his neighbors when he could, supported the local team and attended all of his kids' games, served as a ring steward at the junior livestock show and even went to church on Sunday fairly regularly, except for those "unavoidable absences" during calving time and especially during hunting season.

A cap that fit too tight and way too much higher-level thinking while feeding range cubes off the back of his beat up pickup to scrawny drought-starved cows probably led to Herman's career bum steer.

He had pondered the merits of politics for hours while hauling multiple loads of round bales. One day, in the tweety bird and star-studded aftermath of the come-along handle bonking him on the *cabeza* while he was loading the hay trailer, he arrived at the conclusion that he should try to be one of those "public servants." In a weak moment—or what we might call a misguided career move—were he one of those notoriously fickle Hollywood types, Herman determined to go into politics.

The next time that he was in town to pick up more of the cow feed that he wasn't sure how he was going to pay for, he circled by the courthouse and climbed the stairs to the clerk's office to throw his feed store "gimme" cap in the ring to run for dogcatcher.

Herman wasn't given to bragging, but as the ladies in the clerk's office helped him fill out the paperwork, he modestly commented that he was well qualified to be dog catcher. He had a natural way with critters.—Anybody could see that just by looking at the bashed-in fender the old twisty-horned tiger-striped mama cow had inflicted on his pickup last year at weaning time when his blue heeler snatched her by the nose and things got a little testy.

Herman had managed to catch the blue heeler on the fly after the cow hooked the dog under his shiny new red collar with a horn and launched him right over the pickup bed.—Quite a catch Herman made too, considering he was going at a full run, arms outstretched and whammed head-first into the corner of the portable catch pen right after he gathered in the yelping hound.—Didn't even fumble the dog.

He had staggered back to the pickup to get his rope, spinning round with the grace of a bullfighter just in time for the charging cow to miss his skinny behind and crash headlong into the pickup fender. He threw the dog in the pickup bed and dove in after him. Things calmed down quite a bit when the dog finally quit barking at the cow after she had exhausted herself repeatedly ramming the fender.

While she stood there panting and pawing, Herman got her calf sorted off and loaded into the trailer, then caught up the dog just before his four-legged "assistant" did the belly crawl and grabbed the old gal by the tail.

The blue heeler only needed 15 stitches at the vet's office. Herman talked the vet into throwing in 20 stitches worth of lacing work on the gash in his own head.—No doubt about it, he surely had a winning way with animals—and veterinarians.

Herman figured he ought to be practicing his talent for the benefit of a wider community—and himself. The prospect of receiving a steady dog catcher's salary and benefits to supplement his modest livestock farming income didn't hurt his feelings. Every decent politician knows the first rule is you have to look out for *Numero Uno*.

Campaign cards that he had printed up said it all: VOTE FOR HERMAN, DOGGONE IT!

The campaign went well for almost a week. Only a modest crowd of people bolted from the coffee shop, the feed store, the lumber yard and the post office before he could hand them one of his campaign cards.

Out of nowhere, Miss Kitty filed to run against him.

Herman certainly didn't mind a little friendly competition—right up until his opponent took out an attack ad in the local Boondocks Weekly Gazette stating:

"Hayseed stock farmer barks up wrong tree. Elect Miss Kitty—A vote for Herman invites CAT-TASTROPHE!

Stung by the savage attack, Herman dug deep—using all $14 he scraped together to fire back in the next issue:

" Miss Kitty too catty to corner canines. Dogs gone astray HOWL for HERMAN, and so should you."

The mudslinging reached a new low in the following week's edition—when Miss Kitty alleged:

"Election records show Herman failed to file form K-9, was collared for flea and tick violations."

The media hounded him about the allegations—they were a snarling pack—like a bunch of dogs worrying a bone.

Hurrying to finish his chores one morning late in the campaign—so that he could get into town to chase down more people to hand them cards—Herman was loading yet another round bale on the hay trailer with the come-along.

As he ratcheted a hefty round bale of cane hay and reminded himself that he really ought to invest in a better come-along, the handle slipped and again popped him on the noggin.'

He heard chirping birds, viewed stars in several vivid colors—and amidst the constellations, he saw clearly where he had gone wrong...

" I don't need to be messing in politics to get knocked around," he told himself out loud as he rubbed the egg-sized knot on his head.

Looking about, he saw the blue heeler, busily doing what he did best—irrigating the hay trailer and pickup tires.

"Come on dog.—That old curly-horned tiger-striped cow probably needs company. She may play rough, but at least she shows us some respect."

A Tale of Two Turkeys

The domestic bird can be a study in stupidity. The wild Rio Grande strain is a wily survivor. Both eat pretty good with lots of gravy.

We have come up with "homemade" turkey at the two ends of the spectrum over the span of forty-some-odd Thanksgivings.

At one end of the scale come the barnyard fowl and at the other, the adaptable Rio Grande strain of wild bird—a survivor if there ever was one.

Pity the poor barnyard bird. He is a study in stupidity. That any of them make it to an age and size to end up in the roaster is a wonder.

From his very hatching, he seems to be searching for means of demise. We have seen birds that would never have hatched at all, had the old hen had the final say.

On one occasion, the hen left the nest in the crucial final hours before the eggs hatched. Dad was evidently minding the nest more closely than the old hen. He gathered the not-quite-ready-for-prime-time eggs, brought them to the house and perched them in cardboard boxes over buckets of steaming hot water. In a couple of hours, we had a bathtub full of peeping turkey poults.

Anyone who has raised domestic turkeys knows that you don't start planning on your light and dark meat just because you managed to get them hatched. They can wander around like so many sheep, bunch up in pen corners and smother en masse. Sometimes they will just draw up short and suddenly flop over dead. Heart attack? Who knows?

Poults wander with alarming regularity into the roadway seeking grain and gravel just when a bull hauler is thundering past with a full load or the neighbor kids, with no muffler on their pickup from the way that it sounds, go blasting by.

Maybe these birds have a major hearing defect. For some reason, I don't know why, domestic turkeys can't hear airhorns and unmuffled engines. Apparently, this is in keeping with an inane drive to be reduced to pressed potted meat.

I have seen my share of turkey feathers come floating slowly back to earth after poults took on rural traffic. These birds can hear it thunder, panic and stampede into the corner of the pen, running up one another's backs until the hapless bottom birds are almost as flat as their kin that played "chicken" with passing traffic.

Perhaps the most "imaginative" way that I have seen turkey poults do themselves in is by standing in the driving rain and looking up at the sky until they drown. This was the fate of the majority of the steaming water-hatched birds. Must have been powerfully imprinted upon them at the moment of breaking out of the shell that they came from water, so they must go back to it and attempt to swim upstream.

Miraculously, some birds survive traffic, storms, stampedes, coyotes, skunks, badgers, to reach maturity. They learn to roost out of the reach of most ground-dwelling varmints and they pick up enough grit and greens, grasshoppers and grain to attain decent size.

If they had any notion of a calendar, they would have one more reason to stampede in panic when November rolls around. We'd probably never get one to the oven.

But they don't and one evening after they are roosted, somebody comes along with a flashlight and a hoe handle with a grab hook made of stiff wire on the end of it, blinds a likely-looking tom and snares him down from the perch with an expert lunge of the grab hook at his leg.

By the light of the next morning, this bird that has beaten most of the odds has completely lost his head and is "dressed" for the occasion, plucked clean while suspended from a shed rafter. Within a few hours he will become an acclaimed culinary treat. This may explain why somebody went to all of the trouble to grow him in the first place.

The wild Rio Grande bird is a survivor and adaptor from the moment it hatches. Frequenting river bottoms, grasslands, rolling brush country and tall cottonwood roosts, living on forbs and insects and seeds, scavenging a little grain from broken hay bales when it can, this creature not only gets by, but thrives in spite of coyotes, hailstorms, fire and drought.

On at least a few farms down in the rolling sand country around Roaring Springs, he is much-revered as a savior of crops back when the great grasshopper plague threatened to ruin everything. The wild turkeys gobbled up the problem and grew fat on it.

He is at once coy and showy, particularly in the spring when wooing hens. The wild bird can run as fast as a good horse and is a strong flier when pressed.

A Rio Grande turkey tom is a thrill to hunt. On a couple of occasions, I have been fortunate enough to line up a three-inch load of copper-plated No. 2's from my 20-gauge with the bluish-red head of a wild beard-dragger.

The roasting pan hasn't known the difference between the barnyard bird or the wild one. Thoroughly rubbed down with butter and roasted slowly, either turns a juicy, golden brown.

Whether he's from the barnyard or the back country, the turkey is just one more blessing we ought to be thankful for. Whatever his ancestry, he eats pretty good with dressing and rolls, mashed potatoes and lots of giblet gravy.

Tilth and Tomatoes

Among the great rewards in this journey are feeling life in seed-ready soil and the taste of a vine-ripened tomato with a sprinkle of salt.

It is high time for tomatoes, once the threat of frost is past and the days are getting long and warm.

Adventurous sorts who plant early will be eating tomatoes from the vine by midsummer, but we show-me types prefer not to rush. We want the soil to be warm to the touch before we get stirred up about digging around in it.

Few enterprises can be as frustrating or rewarding as attempting to grow tomatoes. Bugs and diseases lurk out there, just waiting to waste thriving tomato vines. Improved varieties have helped. I can poke some Early Girl sets in the ground and feel reasonably confident that they have a fighting chance.

With tomatoes, you either get a very thin crop that won't fill a bucket or a super one that you cart out by the wheelbarrow full. Despite your best efforts, it is ultimately up to the plants and the season, as to the outcome. Some years are tomato years; some aren't.

There is no reward in all of gardening any greater than a vine-ripened tomato with a sprinkle of salt. It is certainly worth putting some plants out, whether you know if it is a tomato year or not.

Setting tomatoes has to be done with decorum if the young plants are to be properly jump-started. This means using a post hole digger to open the planting sites and filling each hole with water dipped from a five-gallon bucket with a can. While the water is still soaking in, you thump the sets from their containers and poke root clump, potting soil and all down in the goo. Soil is then shoved in and firmed around the young plant, which gets your hands good and mucky. All of this gives the tomatoes a great start and you a sense of whence we came.

To grow things successfully, hand-and-heart contact with the soil is essential. That goes equally for the small garden out back or fields of hundreds of acres.

Watch a lister planter at work, leaving moist, dark soil in its wake and tell me that you're not tempted to sink your hands deep into the seedbed and scoop up a double handful of warm, mellow loam. As they pass, lister planters leave the rich, earthy scent of spring and renewed hope.

Short of a baby, there is probably no other thing that a person can hold in their hands that rivals seed-ready soil for feeling full of the essence of life. Both have so much potential, yet both are fragile and need loving care.

Dad always made lots of stops to dig around behind the planter. Ostensibly, this was to check for correct planting depth, to be sure that the seed was being dropped in good moisture and packed in the seed furrow so that it would be in good contact with the soil and not dry out.

Thinking back on it, this may have been an excuse to get down from the tractor and into intimate contact with the soil, since you had to paw around in the mellow loam to dig down to the seed row. Touching Mother Earth imparted understanding of what we were about. This couldn't be had if all of one's time was spent behind the steering wheel of the tractor.

Feeling the soil in our fingers was a poignant reminder to approach our task with humility. We were at work with the land, small players on a stage so much more vast than what we deemed "our" little acreage. We could play our part well and bring sustenance forth from the good earth while sustaining it, or we could be foolish and let it erode, squandering in less than one lifetime a timeless heritage we held on loan from future generations.

From this we came and to it we will return, all in the good time of life's great cycle.

Dad learned young to understand what the soil was telling him. He will take a handful from down about planting level, roll it around in his hands and squeeze it between thumb and forefinger. If it's gooey, he announces that we are in too big of a hurry to plant—it's too wet. When the soil is moist but crumbles without smearing, it's time to get with planting.

Converting from four-row to six-row farming equipment was a big deal for us. One of the first things we changed over was a planter. Dad hired a local welder to make up the rig from a couple of pieces he bought at an auction.

That spring was made for lister planting. The soil moisture was there and the beds were warm and clean and ready to go.

Dad strung all kinds of drags behind the planter boxes to get the seed covered and packed just right. There were iron and chain drags and he rigged some sack contraptions to drag behind them. Seemed like a parade passing when everything trailed out at a turn.

I don't think I've ever smelled a field as alive, felt it exude as much hope, or seen seedbeds as loamy smooth as the planter and drags left them that spring.

It was a real down-to-earth high.

Dawn and Dusk Magic

Nature compensates for "sweat equity" invested during Plains summer days.

"Sweat equity" is a commodity you literally pour into your enterprise when performing work outdoors in summertime.

Early mornings and evenings make the warm weather season livable here on the High Plains. They bring vibrant sensations and paint gorgeous pictures on the summer air.

When the waking sun is but an orange glow on the horizon, the morning air is cool and pleasant, perfumed with earth and foliage scents.

If the humidity is such that the air is not too dry, crystalline dew will have beaded-up across the ground-hugging leaves and seed heads of Bermuda grass. Your bootprints as you cross the yard are etched in dark green where the silver was trodden in the sparkling dewy grass.

Summer dawn brings a wakening crescendo. Mourning doves coo. Mockingbirds trill and screech, mimic and challenge as their dark-and-white wing flailing moves them along the back fence and into the treetops.

Rustling leaves and the tassels and silks of towering corn plants in the garden are silhouetted against the eastern glow.

In this cool-tinged hour, before the solar furnace is stoked to full flame, you can feel the new life in the day. This prompts wonderment that you have been granted the gift of another day, another chance. This is not unlike the song you sometimes hear at the Easter season—"Morning has broken, like the first morning."

You enjoy the cool freshness while sharpening your hoe, using both hands to guide the ridges of the studded file across the business end of the tool. Many such sessions of edge enhancement have incrementally thinned the cutting edge. Steady metal-to-metal strokes remove shavings, coaxing from the hard metal a keen edge to pit against the task of hacking down an invasion of pigweed and kochia within the garden or the field.

The work begins in the morning cool, the chuff, chuff, chuff of the hoe blade knifing into soil to slash loose the roots of interloping invaders.

Soon enough, within the first couple of hours of the morning, the earth itself begins to bake in the intensifying sunshine. The cool optimism of morning ebbs as heat shimmers distort the distant horizon. Sweat pours.

Tough red-and-green-stemmed pigweed and wiry bluish kochia, smoking with pollen, and reeking devilsclaw yielded easily to the hoe in the morning cool, but seem to have grown more obstinate in the heat, their roots clinging stubbornly to the soil. The vegetative enemy now surrenders only grudgingly to the blade of the hoe.

As the temperature rises, the hacked-loose weeds droop and wither swiftly where they fall. The hoe-swingers droop, too. The water stops are frequent, the task severe, working into the heat of the day.

The hours after dinner are the hardest. With full stomachs, workers are sleepy, the air is still and stifling hot, the progress only tenuous. The tally of finished rows seems a trifling sum, as do the wages weighed against the hours.

With the passing of the afternoon, a reprieve can be sensed. In the still-lighted sun-sinking evening, the rarified edge of a summer day dulls.

Hopeful clouds blossom from scattered wisps—a dramatic backdrop for the descending sun.

Grayish-blue shadows lengthen, light softens, the hum of mosquitos accompanies evening's descent. Streaks of red and orange and yellow meld with shafts of bright-and-gray and blue on the western horizon. On the Plains, the sun retires in glorious-hued riot. This is an unmistakable cue for weed warriors to pile their hoes in the pickup and call it a day.

Just as the evening light mellows, so too does the air. It is as if an oppressive weight is suddenly lifted in the sunset hour. Freshening evening breezes bring revival.

The evening air cools and grows more gentle. With fall of darkness, the stars flicker to life as the Plains night sky hangs out its lanterns. In the ebony-and-indigo bowl overhead, the stars are a friendly light in the mild summer night.

Out in the countryside, while tending to nighttime irrigation or lying in the grass in front of the family farmhouse and peering up at the dippers, or staring up from amidst the bluffs and draws of the Palo Duro Canyon, or adjacent to the channels of the Tierra Blanca or Frio, or Running Water Draw, stars seem much brighter and closer-to-hand in the vastness of the night sky.

The summer night's freshening breezes whisper encouragement to the Plains and its people who have endured another blistering day.

Weather Signs

Nature posts weather indicators at least as accurate as meteorologists come up with.

Weather is "working" more in the High Plains in the spring and summer months than at almost any other time of the year. The clouds boil up quickly to spawn a storm. With the atmosphere mixed-up over whether it is supposed to be warm or cold, any early spring day can offer pleasant climes, howling wind, rainshowers and even snow, all in the space of a few hours. All of that, plus pea-sized hail and lightning, can come out of one cloud.

Once summer gets here, it is supposed to be warmer, but we have seen blustery July days when you needed a coat. You can spot most of the fools and newcomers to this country. Just watch whether they carry along a jacket.

A sultry summer day with a too-hot, foreboding edge sends thunderheads roiling to incredible heights. They puff up in great billows, building upon themselves, and move in quickly. When they bear a dangerous chill, the abrupt coldness portends the presence of dreaded "hard stuff" in the clouds. There is not a wheat or cotton farmer alive who can feel at ease when such clouds are making.

Media weathermen get a lot of advertising about their prognosticating proficiency. They have gadgets to play with in making their guesstimates. Those fancy Doppler radar units may not be dapper when it comes to getting the weather right, though.

If you want an accurate forecast, you'd probably do about as well to take a cue from nature. She posts weather signs for those who look and listen.

Watch for "sun dogs" as a tip-off. These colorations of the evening sky might be likened to mini-rainbows, sans the rain. If seen in the western sky, a "wet" sun dog to the right of the sun portends moisture, but not necessarily a good rain, possibly within three days. A "dry" dog is found to the sun's left. Dogs can also be seen in the eastern sky, where the wet and dry dogs swap sides of the sun. Two sun dogs can be visible at once, but if this occurs the dry side will usually win out over the wet one.

Old Puss can make her weather forecast, too. Observe as she methodically performs her lickdown bath. On-farm philosophy has it that if she licks her paws and makes some swipes behind her ears, it's going to rain.

Frogs croaking in the afternoon are another indicator of impending rain. The croaking is deep and bellicose, not in the cadence you hear when frogs are "blowing bubbles" at night. One of these deep croaks is unmistakable and pretty-much on the money.

Crickets sing of forthcoming rain, holing up in some corner and working a little "overtime" in the morning or afternoon, having not chirped enough the night before.

Pesky flies may suddenly start biting hunks out of you before a shower.

How about a ring around the moon? You don't see these so much in the mild weather months as in the fall and winter. What does it mean? Some believe that a ring around the moon means moisture is on the way. Seems reasonable enough. It takes a fair amount of moisture in the atmosphere to give the appearance of a misty ring surrounding the moon. There is an old saying that a ring around the moon "up close and tight means a shower that night, but if the ring is out a ways, it could be a few days."

When the spider burrows into its nest beneath the window overhang during the day, leaving only a little of its posterior exposed, look for rain within a short time.

An extra layer of shucks on the corn may portend a hard winter—the corn field providing for critters in its own way with additional fodder.

Wooly caterpillars seen abundantly through the late summer may forewarn of a severe winter.

A pig running with a stick in its mouth has sometimes been thought to indicate that a change in the weather is on the way, but it may also mean the pig likes to carry sticks in its mouth. If the hogs start to carry sticks in their mouth and use them to really build up a "sow's nest" of bedding, it could mean either the pig is getting ready to domino or there is some cold weather on the way.

Watch out if the old boar hog begins to make himself a serious nest. A sure-enough blowing snow may be coming. If the boar roots out a place in the center of this nest and beds down, you can almost bet that the storm is going to come that night. The hogs did this just before the famous blizzard of 1957. Blew the barn plumb full of snow, piled drifts up to the rooftops and buried fences all over the countryside. The hogs hunkered down beneath it all.

Dismiss nature's weather signs as superstition and folklore if you like, but the things of nature probably get the forecast right at least as often as the radio and TV guys, if not more so.

About the most accurate method of weather forecasting that I know of is to put your hat on your head and step out the door.

If the hat blows off, it's probably going to be windy.

If water starts dripping off of the brim, chances are it is going to rain.

If snow fills the brim up, look for flurries and flakes.

Thudding sounds and sharp bonging sensations on the *cabeza* say that hail is likely.

If you can't see the hat in your hand—must be foggy.

If the hat casts a shadow, the sun is out; if it doesn't, it's cloudy.

If sweat begins to trickle down from its band, the temperature is warm. Icicles forming on it indicate cold.

Should it get sucked right off of your head and go spiraling upward in a counterclockwise motion, and certainly if you find yourself spiraling upwards with the hat, chickens, assorted barn roofs and the house and contents, you have probably dawdled too long about seeking shelter from an approaching tornado. Still, the hat will probably have given you at least as much warning as you would have gotten from some of those "metroplex" television stations that don't get excited about weather events out in the hinterlands and issue bulletins only when the clouds reach their city limits.

There it is. Simple. Accurate.—Don't forget to take a jacket along. Wouldn't want to come off as a fool, or worse, a Yankee newcomer.

Wind: The trial of March

On a tear, the Plains wind becomes a blustering bandit.

March, ever a blow-hard, gusts all-the-more severely every fourth year with the endless rhetoric and ruminations of politicians aspiring to the presidency. The politicos wax windy, promising so-called answers to questions that they don't understand. Their hot air adds to the turbulence.

In the windy season, you can always recognize West Texans. They have mud on their teeth and around the edges of their mouths.—There is something to be said for the kind of folks who can manage a smile during a wind-driven dirt storm.

No debate in the Capitol can equate with the winds stirring the Plains.

At a whim comes a shift from beneficent breeze to brazen brigand. Treasures of moisture and fragile topsoil are stolen. The Plains wind, on a tear, becomes a blustering bandit, a kick-dirt-in-your-face bully, casting a pall over the sky with its great clouds of dust.

Unbridled, the wind rolls all before it, pillaging a heritage before it can pass to future generations. Tirades of untamed Plains winds are legendary...A whole dark decade, the "Dirty Thirties," was punctuated by ceaseless winds that literally moved an entire countryside about. Soil was thieved in such profusion as to blot out sun and hope.

Upon the Plains, spring winds set the windmill blades and tail fan to such nerve-wracking, protesting revolution and bring about such frenetic clanking of the sucker-rod within the pipe stem, that the whole of the contraption might rip free of its mountings.

The wind could as easily send the wood and aluminum towers and fans hurtling end-for-end as it does the gale-enlivened tumbleweeds. Tower or tumbleweed, the wind cares not. Either is rolled and bounced off to the unknown places where insistent winds go.

The tortured windmill pumps madly. The stream of water from the discharge pipe is wind-blasted into misty spray before it reaches the tub. Clanking work is directed by the gearbox at the top of the tower, in the teeth of the wind.

Blasts of wind whirl gears so rapidly that the rig must surely be torn apart.

The brake, set with tugs of cable, rope, frantic ratcheting of a come-along handle, intercedes between the mill and destruction. The blades must be left free-wheeling in their own distressing whir of air, or be held staunchly against the insistent gusts.

Big blows on the Plains are like Nature's temper tantrums. She is, understandably undecided, confused, frustrated, as to which season to give sway.

Spring will come only when it musters strength enough to shove winter aside and winter will not go easily.

Between the days of fitful bluster come interludes of tranquil warmth and light breezes. They project promise for a time to come.

Rarely, the light breezes may carry the hint of moisture...But the mild, gentle days must be paid for and the winds of March are the toll-taker.

Fitfully, winter makes its last stand, wrestling with spring for supremacy. Cool and warm air collide in banshee-howling tussles. Some years, neither season is a clear winner. Summer takes over by default.

With only windmill towers, barbed wire fences, sprinkler pivots and spotty plantings of trees standing between Canada and the advancing weather fronts that bring gales, the fitful changing of the seasons "wind-tunnel-tests" all that is in and on the Plains.

Those who survive this testing-by-bluster have learned to be like the durable buffalo grass, sinking roots deep and hanging on.

Hail, Hell and Rainwater

There are summer times when fragile crops are in the field, thunderheads boil angrily overhead, and a sinking feeling in the stomach says that the worst is coming.

Sitting and watching the weather is always humbling. No matter how big the tractor or the combine, nor how big you think that you are, our scope is puny next to the elements.

There are summer times when fragile crops are in the field, the air turns deathly chill, thunderheads boil angrily overhead, a smell of savaged vegetation comes suddenly on the wind, and a heavy feeling in the pit of your stomach tells you that the worst is coming.

The first onerous hailstones crash down, striking the ground and bouncing high in the air with the energy of unleashed fury. Ice projectiles painfully thump arms and legs as you shut off the tractor and run for the pickup. They whang against the pickup cab, each hard impact upon the vehicle body jangling nerves already on edge. Every strike sounds as if it must surely shatter the thin glass of the windshield.

Warm and cool air masses have collided within the clouds. Their fierce commingling spawns an icy weather tantrum. Man is powerless to do anything except pray and watch, and it is best not to watch.

The savaging by ice crystals of what had been green and growing hopes is heart-and-soul-rending.

Even though six combines have been in the field running hard to gather the promise, decimation of a wheat crop comes. To hear it happening is brutal enough, but to watch and think on what is transpiring brings only vain effort to understand and comprehend.

Some may manage to be philosophical about a hail-out. They are exceptional people. Waiting for a hailstorm to spend itself is accompanied by thoughts of all of the hard work, resources and promise beaten to hell by spiteful weather. It is hard to think of anything else when the hailstones set up their fearsome din.

Seeing the aftermath is hurtful. Once-thriving cotton plants are toothpicks; corn and maize have been savaged to nubbins. Formerly-majestic seas of amber wheat are reduced to twisted, beaten-down masses of soggy straw. Kernels beaten from the heads are scattered over ground that has been packed hard by the icy hammering.

Any harvesting to be done in a field mauled by hail is most efficiently accomplished with a match, once the straw dries.

When the country is dry and parched, needing rain, and the rain comes, it is delicious to watch a slow soaker coming down, to revel in the sound of it on the roof and the prolonged roll of distant thunder when you are snoozy. It is good to feel and smell and absorb the significance of a gift of renewal that falls from the sky and into our laps. Rainwater brings appreciation for the unexpected pleasure of a couple days off when a timely shower allows shutting off irrigation wells.

Brutal storms and timely, gently-falling showers are both extremes in the Plains country. Usually, weather events are less spectacular in either their damage or their beneficence.

Somewhere amongst the storm events are sun-spangled days that nourish crops and kids in their astonishing spurts of growth, that yield the pleasant odors of new summer mornings, moist earth and flourishing vegetation, dew, new-mown hay, fresh-cut grass, watermelon.

Such days bring appreciation of a good shade tree in the midday heat, enjoyment of the golden summer evenings that dull the edge of the rarified air of the day with the settling of their pleasant coolness. We sit and jaw with neighbors, sip iced tea and cook on the grill in the back yard, feasting on roasting ears and vine-ripened tomatoes, snapped beans and black-eyed peas and charcoal-grilled steaks, chicken and fresh-caught trout.

If the fates are kind and do not deal us too many hands of the hell of hail, if the clouds open and pour forth welcome rain in a timely manner, the Plains can yield such bounty as men are hard-pressed to measure, and summer can taste so sweet—if the fates—and the clouds are kind.

Scare Holes

Some of the storm cellars that folks head for when clouds threaten are pretty scary themselves.

When a big twister hit Friona on June 2, 1995 and was thought to be moving right down Highway 60 towards Hereford, we suddenly became very popular at our house. We have a large "scare hole."

As the storm approached, the driveway in front of the house suddenly looked like the parking lot at K-Bob's Restaurant on Friday at noon. The population of the premises ballooned from three to eleven in less than a minute. Folks showed up with impeccable timing—the Wombles, the Bells, Terry Sparks, Connie Matthews. Their arrival couldn't have been more perfectly choreographed. Everyone was headed down the basement stairs when the tornado siren blew. I took a quick glance out the door to see if any more neighbors were coming and flipped on the porch light as an invitation to head on down.

We found enough folding chairs to supplement a sofa, love seat and some dining chairs and got all of the folks settled. There was an astonishing collection of people, three amazingly well-behaved dogs—and two stuffed toy monkeys.—Any hole in a storm.

We had pretty luxurious accommodations compared to some of the scare holes I have seen that were hollowed with the idea of riding out storms. We sat there with electric light, as thankfully, there was no damage to the power lines, a scanner to give us instantaneous reports from the cloud watchers, a ping pong table, games and toys for the kids and pleasant conversation. Everybody had a flashlight in their pocket—just in case.

Scare hole is a country term, usually associated with a storm or root cellar that is sought-out as a place of shelter during inclement weather and put to other uses the rest of the time. Basements are a much more genteel form of scare hole—concreted and dry and easily accessible right under the house.

Some of the scare holes that rural people head for in a storm might be aptly named for the effect that they have on those seeking shelter in them. Musty cellars may be lairs of spiders and snakes, jumping toads and crawly, creepy, slimy things (real or imagined) that give some folks the willies and cause them to ponder if they wouldn't just as soon take their chances with a tornado.

A lady in Lubbock said that as a girl she and several other shrieking types were just fine-and-dandy going to a dark cellar in the midst of a raging night storm until someone made the mistake of firing up a kerosene lamp. The dim lamplight revealed "slimy salamanders" in the earthen cellar. The shrieking sisterhood nearly had a runaway.

At the farm near Hart, our cellar wasn't bad. It was solid concrete, except for the big wooden door atop it that rested a little above ground level on a cement frame. In the dark, you felt for the shallow steps with your heel, counting your way in the dark when the skies were threatening and you were among the first down there in the wee hours.

The Featherstons, weather-aware neighbors just down the road, often thought the clouds looked bad enough to come to our cellar. More than a few times, their clan and ours gathered, muddy-footed and wet from the dash-in-a-downpour to the staircase, and huddled by kerosene lamplight in the musty confines of our damp-floored cellar. A couple of metal drums and an old grain door supported a mattress where the kids nested. The adults and older kids perched on a work table and a few odd bits of furniture. We waited-out weather's unknowns amongst the shelves filled with cans and jars of fruits and vegetables and odd bits of machinery and parts.

Some hoppy-toads usually thumped around the floor. Anywhere from two to half-a-dozen cats would be sliding in and out amongst us kids.

We would all peer at the staircase, wondering if the world was blowing away up there. Through the cracks in the wooden cellar door, we could see and hear brilliant lightning flashes, the rumble of thunder, the dripping of rainwater onto the concrete staircase from the cracks in the door, the raindrops and hailstones splashing in the yard. It got deathly still up there a few times—and pretty nervous down where we were. One of the men would ease over and hook the big chain from the cellar door to the boomer attached at the bottom of the stairs and dog it down.—I don't know if it would have held, had wind and suction tested it, but a taut, stout chain was reassuring. We out-lasted many storms.

We were lucky we didn't need to go to the cellar the time the rain came so hard and piled up so fast in the yard that the water ran down the staircase and filled the hole with water. Dad set a pump down the stairwell and jerk-started the motor. Water was suctioned out of there in rhythmic surges for a whole day until it got so low that the pump wouldn't pick it up anymore. We went down in irrigation boots with grain scoops and buckets and finished the job.—A grain scoop makes a decent bail bucket in a pinch.

Mom's Uncle Andrew was a hand at concrete work. He redesigned the cellar access with an upright door and a sloping entry-way that did away with the flood-prone ground-level door. A strategically-placed drainage ditch also helped.

Once the cellar entrance precluded the entry of cats, frogs and other varmints, there was a session of whitewashing. Later, windows on the north and south sides were renovated so that water seepage was minimal. The floor got so that it was dry more often than wet. This ended our cellar's stature as a den of musky adventure and took much of the scariness out of the scare hole.

Randy's Roundup

Old-time/modern cattle gathering is worthy of its historic Palo Duro Canyon surroundings.

Whispers of the ancient ones floated on the breeze coming up from the great ravine below. Words were not necessary as we stood in awe on the rim, letting our eyes feast on the changing hues of cedar-dotted clay as daylight waned and shadows lengthened. The Palo Duro Canyon is ever a place of magic and mystery and it was sharing both on this evening.

Our camp, pitched on the canyon's edge, had a scenic overlook of history. The rough-and-tumble land below had been the last bastion of the proud Comanche, the Cheyenne and the Kiowa, an erosion-carved expanse where Colonel Ranald S. Mackenzie had, on September 20, 1874, finally found and attacked their winter camp and snuffed-out the means of one Plains culture to roam and make a living. In the same canyon, Charlie Goodnight had soon launched a new enterprise to fill the void with his first crack at cattle ranching in the Panhandle.

Sprawling for miles below us was holy ground of the nomadic warriors of old. Even Mackenzie's capture and ultimate slaughter of 1,040 of the tribes' beloved ponies within the weather-worn gorge of Tule Canyon to the south could not long still an equine essence of the canyonscape.

On September 23, 1995, in a moving ceremony in Palo Duro Canyon, historic re-enactors representing Mackenzie's old 4th Cavalry presented the Comanche and Kiowa with horses as gifts to restore the horse spirit to the Palo Duro. The Comanche were given a Palomino, and the Kiowa an Irish Cobb. Members of the Cheyenne nation were unable to attend due to tribal business.

Re-enactors honored the Comanche and Kiowa with a saber salute—a tribute traditionally reserved for high dignitaries, presidents and retiring generals.

Jimmy Northcutt, founding member of Company E. 4th U.S. Cavalry Frontier Regiment of the High Plains (memorial), Maggie Johnson of Partners in Palo Duro, Larry Scruggs, Palo Duro Canyon State Park superintendent, and Billy Turpin, president of the Inter-Tribal Indian Organization, formulated the grand idea for the ceremony.

Wallace Coffey, Comanche chief, accepted the gift and pronounced that the ancient ones were watching the ceremony and smiling—and the horse spirit had been appeased. The restored spirit of the horse once again runs free through the canyonlands of old.

As the moon rose over our night encampment, we wondered if we might hear the rumble of Indian pony hooves echoing from below. An enduring legend holds that a ghost herd of Indian ponies periodically arises from the Tule Canyon in the form of thunderheads towering over the gorges, and their hoofbeats can be heard reverberating from red clay walls and cliffs.

The rains had been generous to the Palo Duro country lying all around us. In the canyon's midst, a shimmering thread marked where a stream—alive with water this year—snaked through stands of hardy old cottonwood trees.

Rangeland above the canyon was rank with myriad grasses—green and lush and ample in their largesse for the cattle pastured here, a stark contrast to the rain-starved summer of the prior year.

The cattle moving amongst the grass and mesquite were the reason we had come together here. This was to be "Randy's Roundup," performed in the midst of historic grassland abutting the great canyon and other legendary Panhandle spreads.

Tomorrow there would be a morning ride to gather cows and calves from the big pastures and bring them to the cattle trap. Then there would be all of the work that went with such a time, branding and worming, castrating and vaccinating, performed in the finest of Panhandle traditions, by "neighboring," with folks coming together from miles around just because a neighbor needed help.

Tonight, there was the company of the coals. Lantern light and the glow of a mesquite fire revealed our latest in the eons-worth of campsites on the canyon.

On this evening, neighbors came together to appreciate the talents of campfire cooks, guitar pickers, fiddle players and story spinners. Each were in turn subjected to close examination against the flickering firelight and held in great esteem by those gathered around. Wesley, Laddie and Joe, Nolan and Jim were in rare form on this evening in their string-tickling renditions of long-sung cowboy laments and homespun humor.

This was a re-enactment of history, a canyonside cookout beneath the stars that kept company with practical purpose.

Gathering the cattle the next morning was, I suppose, a lot of grown-ups and some youngsters "playing cowboy." Working the cattle could likely have been accomplished more practically with the aid of catch pens and squeeze chutes, but going horseback was the most efficient way of gathering critters from the mesquite and cedar-studded rough country.

Going too modern just didn't fit here. This work would be done in the old way—neighboring and applying horseflesh and leather and muscle to accomplish the job, while lubricating the industry with humor and camaraderie.

There is still something about a mesquite fire, coffee pots and Dutch ovens and running irons in the coals, a loop well-thrown, heel-caught calves being dragged to the fire, the scramble of hands to the work, that reconnects us to our past and seems eminently worthwhile.

We ride the tamed landscape now in our Range Rovers and 4x4s and SUVs, being far-removed from all of this, yet there are those who willingly give up comfort and even endure no small risk of injury to have a role in reconnecting with the old ways.

To them, the smell of burned hair and the smoke rising as branding iron is pressed to calf hip or shoulder is an incense offering to the days of range riders—their rough traditions mostly gone by.

Things are far more comfortable and convenient now, but there is something about the continuation of a bit of history that is much-appreciated, even revered.

I came to the outing with my camera and hopes of capturing images of the elusive essence of all of this. Lowing cows and calves, spirited horses, ability in the ways of "cowboying" on the part of many of the participants, all of the trappings of the work, have an enduring and endearing mystique.

You meet a decent set of folk around the campfire, tacking-up their horses, pushing-in the cattle, catching heels with their loops, tailing-over the calves, leaning on the fence.

Working in the old way is hard and bruising, even a little dangerous, but those doing it seem accommodating, happy and amazingly at-ease.

A verse from the music of the land rings forth in the sounds of bawling cattle and nickering horses, hard-working neighbors, clinking spurs and creaking saddles, shouts of encouragement and the easy laughter of friendship.

It is enterprise worthy of its timeworn canyon surroundings.

Hay, Hold the Hard Drive

What! No computer? A farmyard proves to be filled with an array of kid-suitable virtual reality.

Recently we had a family gathering at my sister's out in the country down at Ropesville.

Assorted great-nieces and nephews were there, along with parents, grandparents, nieces, and the usual sisterly and brotherly suspects.

The kids, about evenly divided between girls and those other, more unkempt beasts, ranged in age from less-than-two on up to hooliganistic preteens and teenagers.

Though we knew it going in, dinner-time conversation further confirmed that these were all city kids. Their talk was of pickup basketball contests and, more technically, computer programs and games—stuff that quickly went right over my head.

After they had wolfed down roast beef, macaroni and cheese, veggies, cherry cheesecake and chocolate cake, they couldn't find a PC to overload, so they had to resort to going outside to run off some of that sugar rush.

Dashing out the back door in their jeans and shorts and playsuits they had little need of jillion megabyte computers, monitors as big as Buicks, or electronic reality games.

A very kid-suitable virtual reality awaited them in the form of a farmyard replete with two mares, colts at their sides, a few goats, rows of round hay bales stacked next to the barn, a tire suspended from the limb of an elm tree by a rope, the requisite old dog and mama cat, and a sprinkler-irrigated cotton field on the south side of the place.—Just everything most any kid would need to explore and make their own fun.

My assignment was to "loose herd" a very busy almost-two-year-old who certainly believed there was fun to be had around a farmyard.

We wore a path between the corrals and the elm tree. At the corrals, we talked to the "hossies," rubbing their flanks and their velvety soft noses.

We galloped repeatedly to the tire swing to be lifted aboard, to sway and happily sing "Old MacDonald." Our little agrarian asked to get down, then asked to swing again—about 50 times.

Our explorations led us to a pile of cottonseed on the ground—interesting-looking stuff that the little lady deemed "corn," worthy of wagging over to the hossies. So we gathered little fistfuls of it and pursued a long and winding path back toward the corrals, thankfully, spilling as we went, so that by the time we got there, the old worry wart in our duo didn't have to be concerned with the hossies getting hold of cotton seed that they weren't supposed to eat. This worked out perfectly over dozens of trips.

The old mama cat drew the attention of a wide age-range of enthusiasts, all of whom were young enough to get away with trundling the poor beast around like a limp feedsack while receiving nary a scratch. Once she had enough, the fuzzy cat's keen sense of self-preservation allowed her to take advantage of a momentary lapse in the attention of her captors. She nimbly bolted underneath a stock trailer with howling youngsters in hot pursuit.

Some of the slightly older and more adventurous of the cat-chasing company decided romping about on the round hay bales would be a delightful pursuit if they could just figure a way to get up there. What are great uncles good for if not providing a leg-up on fun? As soon as other kids saw what was going on, we had a mob in need of leg-ups and a leaping, howling good time underway on the hay. Even the computer gurus in the crowd found this activity to be fun programming.

My almost-two companion thought we should inspect the cotton field, and so we did. The sprinkler's drops were fortuitously positioned just beyond the reach of an almost-two, so, doggone it, there was no swinging from the dangling pipe and plastic for my little friend.

Underfoot, however, excellent adventure awaited. Small clods turned up by the cultivator were "rocks" worthy of lugging around and periodically exchanging for other rocks. We compared and exchanged and moved a lot of "rock" in a very short time in that cotton field.

The inner farmer in my almost-two charge came out. She grabbed a stick and started poking around in the sandy soil. I think she jabbered something about planting dates and cultivation and short-season cotton varieties, near as I could tell, and I swear, I think I heard her say "need a rain."

Tradin' Pickups

One of life's traumatic experiences is trying to buy
a vehicle without getting skinned alive.
—I'd almost rather visit a dentist.

Don't get me wrong, I'm not knockin' car dealers. We have a couple around here that are solid community citizens. They support the fire department, school sports, academic events, 4-H and FFA, and even the church page in the local paper.

That said, I am not a good auto consumer. I would about as soon take a whippin' as try to trade for a car or pickup. For me, shopping a new or used vehicle lot is about like wading barefoot through a rattlesnake den strewn with a mixture of shattered glass and goat-heads, and rigged with tripwires. One way or another, you're gonna' get hurt.

I am one of those endangered birds who is traumatized by the price of late-model used, let-alone new vehicles, the rantings of salesmen concerning what a good deal they're making me and five-year plans with payments higher than those for my primary abode.

I could pay off our house with money to spare for the sum that vehicles sell for today. Shucks, you could run a small country for the price a luxury SUV commands.

Though I doubt the auto industry has felt my personal trade policy of boycotting ridiculous prices, my purchases have been few, far between, ridden hard, but put up carefully, not wet.

My one and only "new" pickup" was a 1974 model purchased in 1975. While the payments weren't bad by today's scale, they were atrocious by 1975 standards, and the astronomic interest rate certainly got my attention. Sitting across from a glaring banker who levied 13 percent usury left a lasting impression. I've not borrowed vehicle money from a bank again.

Having driven "old Red," the 1974 model, for nearly 30 years, I finally made a radical move and purchased a "newer" pickup recently. I hope I made the right move.

The "new" rig is nothing extravagant—a 1990 Ford F-150 regular cab, maroon in color, that had just rolled over 100,000 miles. Carrying about half the miles on Old Red, the 1990 cost close to what I paid for the 1974 model new.

I was feeling like I had betrayed an old friend as I cleaned out the cab of the red Ford after bringing the maroon interloper home.

My old pickup took me through a lot of experiences and to a lot of places.

It hauled loads of hogs to help me make a buck, trailers full of duck blinds, duck and goose decoy spreads, crates of pheasants, furniture when we moved into our first rent house, our first home, and the one we're still paying off now.

I hauled the entire press run every week in my first newspaper job at the Castro County News—first from the printing plant in Hereford back to Dimmitt, then over to the Dimmitt post office after labeling, sorting and bundling.

My wife and I went on our first date in that pickup, back in the day when the Viking Red exterior was still bright and the rig hadn't collected many dents of experience.

We borrowed a camper shell to cover our possessions and drove it to Colorado on our honeymoon.

Fitted with a camper shell of our own, old Red took us to Yellowstone Park twice. We tailgate picnicked with elk moving through the timber right behind the pickup. Swarms of mosquitos kept us from lingering long.

I drove the red Ford along the Yellowstone River and found an inviting stretch where I tried fishing with a dry fly for the first time.

A road trip with Mom in the pickup happened a while after our daughter, Jaime, was born. We stayed in South Fork, Colorado. One of the locals put me onto a hike-in adventure on Trout Creek. The pickup got me to the trail head where the sign claimed it was three miles to Trout Creek—must have been as the crow flies.

Once I finally reached the creek though, the brown trout there took my Adams and elk hair caddis flies aggressively. I landed six, then got back on the trail to pack out well before dark.

I was tired and sore and glad to see the red rig when I rounded the last bend in the trail and spotted the parking area.

My daughter Jaime rode with me in the pickup on adventurous outings. We visited John A. Smith's place to see cows at the feed bunks when she was a toddler. We dropped in at the Carlson place to see Lawrence and Betty Jo's barnyard critters—chicks and ducklings, goslings and baby calves, when she was in kindergarten.

In one of the Carlson's fields we attempted to find the perfect pumpkin while Jaime was in grade school.

We gathered fodder for feed shocks to serve as Halloween and Thanksgiving decorations out at Hagar Hill.

There was one year, during the county's big Jubilee celebration, that we rigged the pickup with some camouflage netting, several giant goose decoys and signs, and drove it as a "float" in the hometown parade.

In the wake of 9/11, once we got our college coed safely back from Washington that November, we had her home for a prolonged holiday break. Just like the old days, we shared an outing to the pumpkin patch—this time out to Larry Malamen's, where we gathered scores of bright pumpkins to decorate the porch and yard. We had a great time just being together and gathering stuff for a harvest theme.

I used the tailgate repeatedly as a workbench—there's a nick from a saw blade there as proof of one of my carpentry goofs.

The tailgate was a bird cleaning table many scores of times and a work table for cooking out on the driveway.

Over the years I've hauled enough pheasant hunters around in the back to constitute a sizable army. When Beau, the faithful Labrador retriever, was less than a year old, Red hauled him to his first pheasant hunt. He's ridden in a crate in the back of the pickup, headed for bird hunting outings, ever since.

The pickup hauled me to canyons and high country in quests for mule deer and elk.

Just a few years back, I rigged long-staffed Texas and U.S. flags on either side of the bed of Old Red. Kerrie printed neat posters with icons and military unit emblems recognizing family community history and military service that we attached to the pickup's sides. Dad rode with me on that day of celebrating families in the Labor Day parade down at Nazareth. There we were, riding in style, two country boys with elbows out the open windows, tooling along the streets of greater "metropolitan" Nazareth like we were somebody. Though Dad served his country in combat in the Asiatic/Pacific theater during World War II, he was not one of those for whom parades and celebrations were staged upon his return. This was his first parade—he pronounced it the best one he'd ever been in. It was great getting to be there with him in the decked-out red Ford.

I guess you're not supposed to get sentimental over machines—yet I don't see this as any different than having a warm spot for a Popping Johnny or a '57 Chevy.

Old Red was a means to joyous experience and adventure for many years.

Hope the "new" pickup is as good and that I didn't screw up the economy by making an impulsive auto buy.

Following Precedent

Centuries-worth of travelers and settlers setup shop where the water was—on Tierra Blanca Creek.

More than a century ago, my wife's grandfather, Troy Womble, may have been speculating about where the Santa Fe Railroad would come through, but he was also following centuries of historical precedent when he established a dugout adjacent to Tierra Blanca Creek. His living quarters was a dugout—a hole excavated in the ground, with a roof protruding above the soil line. Back in 1898, he did the same thing that nomadic Indians, hordes of explorers, traders and assorted opportunists, maybe even Paleo-era man had done; he setup shop where the water was.

Troy probably didn't have any idea back then that the area where he established a semi-sunken abode would become present-day Hereford. Jabs of his spade that peeled away sod and created his dwelling cavity set in motion a century of evolution.

Although the trend of his day had been to go deeper west into Deaf Smith County to settle, Troy was well-aware that it was a whole lot easier to haul water only the short distance from the creek to his dugout than it was to freight it many miles into the water-short western interior. It wasn't long until others were moving back, closer to water at the creek, too.

Portions of Tierra Blanca Creek and its surroundings that are now suburbs of Hereford have been important to beast and man, probably since prehistoric times. Down through history, the creek served not only as a source of water, but as a sort of road map that didn't have to be folded.

Rising in eastern New Mexico, Tierra Blanca Creek snakes into Deaf Smith County on the south side, depending solely on rainfall for its sustenance from its origin through Parmer County, to near the center of Deaf Smith County. At a point roughly 25 miles inside Texas, the creek bed cuts into Tertiary deposits and springs that once fed it constantly, although, sadly, they don't today.

As Hereford celebrated its 100th birthday, the community could look back to a time when springs were once notable along the creek adjacent to the city. Surfacing as clear blue holes, springs were found where the city golf course, the pro shop and the Main Street highway bridge are now located, and they helped to sustain a flowing creek.

Tierra Blanca Creek has played its role not only in the history of Hereford, but the Panhandle.

Tepee rings of ancient nomad tribes and the bones of long-gone buffalo are found above and within its banks—talismans of its history.

Ruts were worn into its banks by the *carretas* of traders, *ciboleros* and *comancheros*.

Leading an army contingent eastward across the Llano Estacado in 1541, *Francisco Vasquez de Coronado* camped in a canyon on the Llano's eastern edge. Some historians speculate that Coronado may have followed the Tierra Blanca while crossing the Plains. The Tierra Blanca reaches a confluence with Palo Duro Creek northeast of Canyon, forming the Prairie Dog Town fork of the Red River that flows eastward through Palo Duro Canyon.

In 1787, *Jose Mares*, on a journey from Santa Fe to San Antonio, apparently crossed the Llano along Tierra Blanca Creek, emerging at Tule Canyon to the east. He retraced the path on a return voyage to Santa Fe in 1788.

Pedro Vial again followed Tierra Blanca Creek to cross the Panhandle in 1789 on a trek from Santa Fe to Natchitoches.

A force led by Captain *Francisco Amangual* out of San Antonio crossed Tierra Blanca Creek en route to Santa Fe in 1808.

Captain J.S. Sutton's ill-fated Texan Santa Fe expedition crossed the area in September of 1841, reaching Tierra Blanca Creek near the Deaf Smith/Randall County line. The main party of the expedition reached Tierra Blanca Creek, about 15 miles east of Hereford, on September 23, then followed the creek out of the Panhandle into New Mexico.

In 1872, looking for cattle thieves and hostile Indians, Colonel Ranald S. Mackenzie led an army expedition that found a wagon road along Tierra Blanca Creek. The main command followed Tierra Blanca creek to its confluence with Palo Duro Creek, likely right through the site of present-day Hereford, maybe even across the area that is now South Main.

Today, the expeditions mounted along the creek adjacent to Hereford are in the shadow of great grain elevators and are essentially made up of duffers engaged in cow pasture pool, beating golfballs around a manicured grassland. They travel on foot, hauling bags of weapons or in battery-powered *carretas*, that continue to rut the perimeter of the creekbed.

This is what history comes to?

Irrigated Irony

Irrigation ditches were the only streams and rivers known by many Plains farm kids.

Amazing how in this arid land, where the growing season is often not generous with its rainfall, much of our everyday life during summers growing-up on the farm revolved around the sounds and sensations of water that flowed for irrigation.

Crops of corn and cotton and maize, sugar beets and soybeans and forage could grow and prosper in lush abundance because we had irrigation.

For this blessing of irrigation to occur, there had to be roaring motors and whining gearheads whose din was so constant that the sound was missed should these implements of lift suddenly fall silent. These machines magically, but expensively, brought forth from deep below the earth the splash of full pipes of water, carried to its work in ditches.

Ditches flowing with cool, clear irrigation water were a farm kid's playground. A place to float wooden boats on a string, to wade and splash and flop and squish bare feet in glorious mud, to chunk dirt clods and make great geysers, a cooling bath to roll a couple of watermelons into for keeping until an afternoon break from cotton hoeing.

The same ditches were an instrument of much grinding labor—slogging in mud, placing ditch stops, shoveling endlessly, setting tubes, hauling tubes, setting more tubes.

As we came to understand the staggering loss of water to evaporation from open ditches, economic necessity dictated that practicality would reign. We resorted, where we could, to virtually unseen distribution of the wet stuff into underground concrete delivery systems. The only real hints that the wells were pumping were their noise and perhaps a trickle of water out the top of a standpipe, or squirts and seeps out air valves and risers along the pipeline route. Through the wonder of underground pipe, water could travel halfway across the farm and resurface, artesian-like, out valves wheeled open to feed eight-inch gated aluminum pipe.

The underground rain's journey in this mode was far less dramatic and visually pleasing than the cool, clear-running flow down the ditch, though more practical and less wasteful in its journeys through concrete and plastic. Even without the ditch, the labor was still there: Hauling pipe, setting pipe, opening valves for one set, hauling still more pipe for another, and mosquitoes chewing up your elbows when your arms were full of tubes or pipe.

Sending water to the waiting fields channeled liquid life through an intricate delivery system of ditches and pipe and finally, down furrows between rows of crops, leaves twisted with urgent thirst. We sometimes thought, on rarified July and August days, that we were tending pineapple fields, rather than expanses of grain sorghum, when leaves rolled up in brown-toned, emaciated cones of compact protest over their dire need for water.

Nothing sounded or felt quite like walking up on an irrigation set that had run long enough so the ground around it was wet and the air coming off the damp ground was noticeably cooler on a summer day. Plants that had drunk their fill had relaxed from their earlier shriveled twist of desperation and were again full-leafed and verdant.

The sound of water running from the gated pipe came with a rush that told how the lengths of aluminum had carried life to the crop again.

Even today, with far more efficient sprinkler system delivery of irrigation—there's still that familiar, bubbling, rushing sound of water released at its point of need, the smells of moist soil and leafy crop, and the feeling of refreshing coolness where the underground rain works its magic.

History's Perspective

*We are struggling to learn a hard lesson:
Some portion of a great gift was squandered
and the future of what is left is limited.*

For almost as far back as I can remember, the song of summer in High Plains farm country has been the close-up roar or the far-off drone of hard-working irrigation engines.

The music has come in different pitches—the steady growl of Chrysler industrials, the hum of Olds and Chevy, Ford and IH powerplants, the rhythmic, throaty purr of well-tuned Molines.

A piston-pounding symphony has mounted and ebbed on the whims of the morning and evening breezes down through the summers.

The combustive power of engines is harnessed to evoke a high-pitched whine from gearheads. For decades, these metal mules have lifted the "underground rain" of the Ogallala aquifer to the surface to slake the burning thirst of the Plains. Up close, their hot blast-in-your-face exhaust was deafening to me while checking the oil and coolant levels and the flow of drip oil to the gearhead. At a far-end-of-the-field distance the muffled rumble was like sweet music when, seated with your Dad in the shade on the running board of the pickup, you were waiting for the long-traveling water. The underground rain had to traverse one side of the quarter-section and build sufficiently in the ditch before the irrigation set could be made.

That was a time that seems impossibly long ago yet serene in its own way now. The labor of setting ditch stops, moving tubes and wading muddy ditches was intense and the mosquitos gnawed your arms and elbows fiercely.

In the ditch-watering days the mark of achieving young manhood came when you could finally set a two-inch siphon tube successfully. There was a knack to it—dunking the tube in the ditch, cupping your hand over the aluminum end, pumping it a couple times till water hissed and throwing the tube down in the furrow. Success came when the tube siphoned water from the ditch and poured it upon the endless rows of thirsting corn and maize and cotton.

Lately, time and deeper understanding of the finite nature of a priceless resource seem to lessen the sweetness of bygone growing season reverie.

Where once the drone of irrigation engines was a confidence-builder, even a soothing evening tune, today it can evoke concern, for it might also be heard as the feeding frenzy of mechanical vampires sucking lifeblood from beneath the earth far faster than it can be replenished.

Back when irrigation was developed on a large scale in the High Plains from the 1930's through the 1950's, the Ogallala was virtually regarded as an instrument of manifest destiny. Plains folk told themselves they had been gifted with an inexhaustible water source that would forever hold drought at bay, supply domestic needs and allow production of bumper crops virtually every year—whether it rained or not.

What was once buffalo and antelope range in the High and Rolling Plains became intensively cultivated farmland. A life-style based on irrigated agriculture evolved into a powerful driving force in the region's economy.

Irrigation techniques during the 1950's, 1960's and even into the early 1970's reflected the assumption of an unending water supply magically provided to us by a "great underground river."

With 20/20 hindsight, we now see that the salad days of full-piped gushers from ten, eight and six-inch wells poured out the richest reserves of the aquifer to irrigate crops yielding surplus harvests of ridiculously underpriced commodities.

In economic terms, producers often received pitifully little return on the commodities they grew compared to the quantities of priceless water expended to make the crops.

During the same lifetime in which we saw irrigated agriculture become a mainstay of the Plains, we slowly came to appreciate that the Ogallala is not an unlimited water supply. Its reserves have steadily been depleted by hard and not-always-stewardly use through the years. Once-gushing irrigation wells that now trickle confirm these concerns.

In the span of a single lifetime, we've seen a major transformation in how we perceive the Ogallala aquifer, the source of the irrigation water that helped transform the region into a verdant landscape. Ogallala water has become a treasure to be guarded closely and sold much more dearly.

All of this is not intended as a roundhouse criticism of the irrigated agriculture that developed on the Plains. Irrigation allowed cultivation of crops where their production would have been only marginally successful otherwise. Rural communities and their economic base came to be with the help of irrigation. Through the years, the great resource of underground rain made it possible for those working the land to keep the banker at bay, and the tax man at least at arm's distance.

Elmer Kelton, the consummate West Texas historical novelist from San Angelo, penned a telling observation on the heritage of the Texas Plains in the introduction to his outstanding novel "The Wolf and the Buffalo."

Kelton maintains "It is unfair to judge past generations by the standards of our own time, any more than we would like to be judged by whatever standards may exist a hundred years from now."

His thoughts were in the context of events such as the conflict between the white man and the Comanche and the slaughter of the vast Plains buffalo herds, but they may also overlap our time.

Kelton maintains that the principals in events behave according to the standards of their cultures within their respective era.

What becomes of the remnant of the Ogallala aquifer will be a reflection of the standards of our own Plains culture.

Future generations who look back on our time from the vantage point of theirs probably won't think highly of our usage of so much water to grow commodities that the country already had in surplus. In the context of the times in which it happened, consuming irrigation water was a means to the end of economic survival.

That certainly shouldn't let us off the hook.

In recent decades, technology and science have helped agriculture get better at using groundwater efficiently, and we should do no less than to use every drop wisely.

Unfortunately, a large portion of a great gift was squandered. We know all too well now that the future of natural resources is not limitless. Our culture is working harder today to conserve and stretch what remains of our treasure.

Economic survival, weighed against the diminishing future of the aquifer, makes for a daunting ethical struggle.

Perhaps we can still write a chapter in the history of our region that future generations will not label as a period of ruinous squander.

I hope that we will have wised-up in time, that we manage what's left of a precious resource judiciously enough that future generations won't be tempted to feel ashamed and label us wasteful.

Red-Top Cane

This colorful Plains forage has performed yeoman service as cud for boys and bovines.

Redtop cane is as much a part of the fall as frost.

Rowbinders once ran through the fields of cane, spewing bundles of sweet fodder to be propped up in shocks.

Now, the big baling machines do the bundling and binding and shocking in a single pass, dumping round bales to cure where they drop in the field. Nearly a ton of cow feed is bound in a cylindrical package with nylon twine. A lot of grinding work is saved in all of this, at the expense of some of cane's folklore.

Much to be liked about redtop cane is chewing it. Small wonder cows love the stuff; it has a uniquely sweet savor of fall.

Cane is hardy, waiting for water better than thirstier crops. Redtop yields something of cow-filling fodder and sweetness amidst bitter fortune. This forage can sugar up suffering through a summer on less-than-enough rainfall while growing on land rife with rocks, goat-heads and bindweed.

Some folks say that chewing cane is good for you—settles the nerves.

There was nothing too nerve-wracking about taking the single-shot .22 out of the closet, stuffing a handful of cartridges in a pocket, whistling up the dog and heading out to the cane patch.

An uncomplicated matter, walking up to a tall stalk, bent with the weight of its dark red grain head, the leaves just turning, and cutting the stalk close to the ground with a pocketknife.

The joints of the stalk marked the length of each section to be cut before the tough outer stem was peeled back with the knife.

Inside, the pulp was a light yellow that oozed juice. Just bite off a piece and chew. Once the sweetness was gone, the pulp was spat out and another chunk bitten off.

Pretty calm stuff, chewing a little cane, kicking around the weedy fencerows and the old post piles for a cottontail out catching the last of the day's sun, or lying flat on your back, watching and listening to the ducks and cranes speeding past overhead.

The shocked cane could become a natural blind to climb into, shotgun-in-hand, and hide from waves of incoming green-headed mallards, chuckling and chattering over all of the grain awaiting in the shocks. From the cane shock hide, it was no great shakes to drop nice braces of the green and chestnut and canvas-colored mallards pouring in.

In the cane patch, small gray field mice scurried as bundles were picked up to load on the wagon. The field crew dodged mice so that the rodents wouldn't scoot up the inside of their pants legs and unleash a jumping, hopping, pants-shucking maelstrom.

Wise field hands remained watchful for skunks that liked to den-up in the hollow inside of the shocks.

Unlike the cane, those polecats didn't have anything to bestow that could remotely be considered sweet.

Indian Summer

Indians regarded this season as a gift from the god of the Southwest...How right they were.

Fall is a fabulous time of change. Among this season's best features are the ocher-tinted days of Indian Summer.

American Indians called this period of mild weather during the fall the special gift of the god of the Southwest, *Cautantowwit*. How right they were.

In Poland, mild autumn weather is referred to as *God's Gift to Poland*. What a Divine endowment, this time of brisk mornings that mellow into pleasantly warm afternoons, then chill into one-blanket, sound-sleeping nights.

It is an inspiring time punctuated with riotous color that rivals spring's display. We are surrounded by pumpkin orange, red-and-purple-and-light Indian corn, golden-yellow field corn, red-topped sorghum, the browns and rusts of turning leaves.

Crops are gathered under a harvest moon that bathes straw-colored fields in a benevolent light so bright that running lights may not be needed. This yellowish-orange orb is incredibly huge, rising so close-by that we feel we could reach out from the tractor or combine cab or the top row of bleachers at the football stadium and shake hands with the friendly-faced fellow smiling on high. We gawk in wonderment at this spectacle of gentle light rising on the night air of the season.

Night chill permeates watermelons gathered from the garden and piled in the shade of low trees. They keep as well as in any refrigerator, yielding cold red or yellow meat when split open with a pocketknife by a youngster just-off the school bus, book-weary and not eager to be confined by four walls for what is left of the daylight hours that beckon one outdoors.

Not too many years ago, Indian Summer brought the days of hand-gathering the leftover field corn from the patch planted for roasting ears. Some school friends or the neighbor kids from down the road would help. We would pick one row at a time, snapping the ears from the brittle stalks and tossing them at a cotton trailer with nailed-together scrap lumber for sideboards. The trailer was kept rolling along at a pace slightly faster than a crawl by our "egg-gathering" tractor, a Massey-Ferguson 65.

Accurately-thrown ears would bang against the sideboard and plop into a growing mass on the trailer bed, the winter supply of hog feed steadily growing as we picked.

The work proceeded briskly in the mornings. After dinner we were less enamored of the labor, our stomachs full, our pace slowing. The mild afternoons made us sleepy. We would often stop the tractor and all pile onto the corn-laden wagon for a rest, taking a cue from my Dad, who frequently allowed how "a hog don't need to be in no hurry. All he has to do is eat and sleep." We figured that the hog feed gatherers weren't in a race either.

Sprawled amidst rustling shucks, we would lie on our backs and stare into the clear blue. Only a short distance above us there were often hordes of migrating hawks, circling in search of mice flushed from their hiding place beneath the corn fodder by the progression of our work.

Incredibly higher up, so far-off that we had to squint to see them, were tiny specks that were migrating flights of sandhill cranes. We heard them before we saw them in the October sky, their prehistoric-sounding cries carrying before them as they spiraled effortlessly on the autumn afternoon thermals. Their flights would set us to speculating on how high up they were, and how long it would take them to reach Muleshoe. Pleasant, lazy afternoons.

Sometimes, the cool mornings of Indian Summer treated us to fascinating mirages. It seemed we were atop a slope, looking down on places that had crept close overnight. We might see the city of Hart, only four miles to the south, as clearly as if it were in our back yard. The elevators of Dimmitt Wheat Growers might seem just down the hill, or the spire of the Holy Family Church and the water tower at Nazareth, six miles to the north, might shimmer close-at-hand. Even the Tulia Livestock Auction or the grain bins at Kress, both a good number of miles distant, might look only a short jaunt away.

We can see and smell and feel the crackling crisp presence of Indian Summer and taste it in freshly-pressed sweet cider and the pleasant sharpness of golden Jonathan apples, cool and crisp as they come from the tree. It is an invigorating time as bounty is gathered against the winter to come.

Just as this brief time is ending, on a night with the hint of a north wind, comes a true sign of the turning of the season.

High-pitched, sharp yelps are suddenly audible above the sound of the television and the clatter of washing supper dishes.

It takes a few seconds for the sound to register. Once the ear distinguishes this ancient beckoning, you go tearing out the back door, soggy dishtowel still draped over your shoulder, to stand in shirtsleeves and sock feet in the chilly night air.

A symphony of fall is being played. With haunting barks, a "V" of migrating geese is suddenly silhouetted against the yellow face of the rising moon. Your heart quickens, your breath coming in white plumes against the frosty air.

Revel in the passing of Indian Summer. The harbingers of fall have come.

Bracing Days

The bracing days as the seasons change are a timeless constant in our lives, even in this uncertain age.

Come September, then October, and the snap is in the morning and evening air, the fine afternoons are clear and pleasantly mild shirtsleeve weather. The full moon's rise in the evening is never more hugely orange and close-at-hand than it is now. The magical days of Indian summer and early fall are upon us.

Spring is a time of new life, but these days too, when the seasons change and the fierce heat of summer refreshingly subsides, are a period when it is easy to feel more alive in the Plains country.

October brings the gathering in earnest of the fruits of spring and summer's toil in the fields and gardens.

Ocher corn fields yield up their yellow grain in the waning days of September, the ramrod-straight soldier stalks giving up the ripe ears to the ravenous combines.

In the mottled tan-and-green expanses of sorghum fields, berries in the ripening heads take on a rust-red or creamy hue in the days before they will be threshed.

Sprawling cotton fields fairly burst into a blizzard of fibrous white from the opening bolls.

The frost will soon be ending their run, but for now the green-hued tangle of tomato plants in the garden behind the house recline against the ground under their load of fruit that turns riotous red when allowed to mature on the vine.

Plucked from their hangout, ripe homegrown tomatoes are about as close to perfect as they can get when quartered and dashed with salt, or in full-colored slices heaped atop most anything that will make a sandwich. How well they team with crispy strips of bacon.

Pouring forth from the garden by the bucket and basketful, full-ripe tomatoes are the raw product to be blended with onions and bell peppers, spices and jalapenos in a simmering pot to compose the nectar of the

Southwest—picante sauce. This elixir of the fall harvest can be stored courtesy of Mason or Kerr, to be called upon at a future date to melt away the cold of the coming winter.

A snap in the air gives an edge to the crisp, tangy apples gathered from local orchards. No mushy pulp here. The taste test proves they are the real deal.

I remember October afternoons, coming home from school to savor the essence of fodder and harvest time on keen air that pulsed with its own vitality.

In the front yard, well-insulated within the shade beneath the juniper bushes where they were stashed, black diamond watermelons hauled from the patch in the field demanded attention. The dark rinds still held the chill of the previous evening and the brisk morning within them.

A few strokes of the pocketknife and an after-school melon oozed with the sweet flavor of fall to be savored by the dog and I.

After having spent much of such glorious days in the classroom, I didn't mind that after-school chores of lugging bucketfuls of water and forking ears of corn to the hogs awaited.

In the October afternoons when the combines were gobbling up the clustered pods of soybeans from their stems after the leaves had fallen, there was also the diversion of climbing aboard the old Case tractor and disking-in the soil-renewing plant matter of the just-harvested beans, before wind could steal the bounty.

October's small-town football Friday nights fairly spark with electricity. What says fall more than a good high school football game on a crisp night with the hometown throng packed into the stands in noisy support and that big old yellow moon rising as a backdrop to the stadium lights?

A part of the October spectacular that lets all of us be a kid again is a trip to the pumpkin patch, where thousands of the orange orbs of fall lie scattered in an awesome technicolor spectacle. Hefty chunks of fall wonderment await in such fields.

There are few timeless constants in our lives. The bracing days of October rank among them.

Wondrous Rituals

As machines lay-in the bounty, winged harbingers are the colorful and timeless vanguard of a new season.

In the years when the rains are generous and the seasons are kind, fall brings wondrous rituals to the Plains.

Insatiable combines gobble up the corn that grew tall and green on the warmth and moisture of the salad days of summer, then blanched to ocher with mellow Indian summer.

Bins gorged, the combines spew streams of yellow and white grain into waiting trucks, loading them brim-full with whole-kerneled wealth to be hauled via turnrows and country roads to the highways and on to the circular concrete high-rises to be banked away.

Ravenous even after their feeding frenzy in the corn, the combines lumber into sorghum fields where green and brown-leafed fodder is topped with endless columns of rusty-red ripened grain heads held high by their stalks at soldierly attention.

Revolving reels gather the berry-laden heads into the machines. Choking clouds of itchy chaff and dust mark the paths of threshing-on-the-go.

Cackling, gaudily-colored cock pheasants and mottled brown hens flush pell-mell from field ends as the giant riveted reapers roust them from sorghum-secreted refuge.

Snowy drifts flash in dark-leafed fields. A final succession of mild days coaxes the last reluctant cotton bolls to crack a fibrous smile.

Amidst the frantic harvest rush to gather before winter can ruin, the sky above the bustling machines is also busy with a profusion of timeless fowl migration. Ragged skeins of geese, fast-flying clouds of ducks, loose strings of sandhill cranes weave their signature across the orange and amber and crimson of dawn and sunset in flawlessly choreographed fall flights.

These flocks have no need of man's calendar. They carry internal datebooks. Southward sojourns are masterfully keyed by day length and light level. With impeccable timing, wildfowl arrive to sing a frost-tinged serenade that prompts shivers not only from the cold, but from the electrically-charged spectacle accompanying the yellow rising of a fall full moon.

On a late autumn afternoon in the Texas Plains, a mild norther blusters notice of its arrival. Yellowed apricot and elm, corn and sorghum leaves are whipped aloft in spiraling minor whirlwinds.

A distant trill of cranes accompanies the rough-and-tumble rustle of the wind-stirred leaves.

The traveling call of a sandhill crane is unmistakable, riveting. We pause from the work of building blinds or slathering Canada goose gray decoy paint on the boat in preparation for the fast-approaching duck season, to peer into the intensely-blue sky. In their thermal-riding rituals, migrating cranes soar impossibly high. They must surely travel in the thin air at the edge of the atmosphere. The eye perceives them merely as specks.

A dozen sandhills pass low enough to be well-observed. They are prehistoric-looking, all neck and legs and wings protruding from bodies of brownish-gray.

They coast effortlessly on the tireless glider wings that carry them in ageless pilgrimage to the South Plains. Their rolling calls confirm on this fall day that the cycle has come full circle. Winged creatures have traversed a year, journeys north last spring to nest, south now to winter, returning once more with the fall. We peer in deference to their perpetual persistence, these winged harbingers. Dusky gray cranes, green-headed, canvas-gray-and chestnut-bodied mallards, dark brown and flashy white long-tail-sprigged pintails, black and gray-bodied and white chin-strapped Canada geese are pouring southward—as they have for all of the generations that men have stopped to stare at the sky, wonder at wildfowl and feel excitement leap in their hearts.

Flights have fluctuated so greatly from year to year at the whimsy of Nature's moisture that we have wondered if the wildfowl would survive at all. In the space of a couple of decades, we have seen their hatches soar and dwindle. Sometimes there is still a good year and the birds are many again.

Winter lies somewhere behind—in the slipstream of the undulating flights that are the vanguard of this new season. It has been left for the moment, perhaps in the Canadian parklands, on the prairies of the Dakotas or along the Platte River in Nebraska. A norther will bring winter soon enough.

In times pockmarked with uncertainty, when we may have lost bearings, sense of direction, tradition, a holiday of meditation and thanksgiving comes, fittingly, when the flocks are on the wing. We welcome the color and the spectacle of trilling, gabbling, quacking, chattering, honking, clamoring winged hordes that have unfailingly made yet another return.

Picking the Corn Patch

The sensation, spectacle and the taste of fall days in October makes a farm boy feel very much alive.

When the Indian Summer afternoons of October come rustling in with a mild and pleasant coolness on the heels of nippy mornings, I always think on days spent years ago picking field corn from the remnants of the roasting ear patch.

Dad usually planted field corn to the west side of the house in late spring. He would make a round-and-a-half or two rounds with the M Farmall and the four-row planter. The rows, running north and south, would be laid off right at the edge of a field of whatever was being cropped that season—sorghum or beans or cotton. The corn patch could be cultivated right along with the regular field crop and watered by setting siphon tubes from the irrigation ditch whenever needed.

Once the number of summer days and the height of the corn plants had grown sufficiently, the shuck-sheathed kernels reached early milk stage and we could wander out to the field to gather fresh corn just 30 minutes before dinner-time whenever we wanted.

Even if we harvested roasting ears heavily, there would still be a lot of corn left out there because the kernels rapidly dented and got too mature to use for the table, canning or freezing.

We seemed to always have a few hogs around as an efficient means of keeping farm boys in chores and as a source of a meager-but-important sum of "possibles" dollars that occasionally were available when pigs ate themselves into top hogs before getting hauled off to the Farmer's Hog Market in Plainview.

The abundance of mature corn that remained in the roasting ear patch was a cheap source of feed for those hogs—reason enough to gather what was left.

Hand picking the eight or twelve or sixteen half-mile long rows of corn would usually take place sometime in early October. The job called for brothers and sisters, neighbor kids, if they were available, and sometimes, a couple of school friends to make up the work crew.

We scrounged up a flatbed trailer, fitting it with two end pieces and a sideboard made from salvaged lumber. One long side was left open so that we could toss the ears of corn onto the trailer unobstructed.

Dad's little Massey-Ferguson 65 "egg-gathering tractor" was the perfect rig to pull the trailer. Set in low gear in low range, the 65 crept along at a slow shuffle—just about right for keeping alongside the corn picking crew.

We could take turns steering the tractor while the others picked. If the water furrows were deep enough to hold the front tires well, you could even get down off the tractor and walk alongside it to do some picking, and still get back up on it to correct the steering if needed.

As we crept along we snapped off ears from standing stalks, salvaged them from the fallen ones and pitched them on the trailer, bright yellow grain and red cobs protruding from the ocher shucks. Progress was measured by the steadily growing pile of corn in the trailer bed. A big corn yield meant pulling out of the field when only partially through to haul in a load to the south side of the hog pen. The ear corn would be forked off into a wired-together picket crib. When the trailer was empty, we would head back to pick up where we left off.

For Mr. Allergy-Prone here, picking the corn patch was not a task to be undertaken without some sneezes, sniffles and sinus headaches.

Yet to this day when too-hot summer relaxes its hold, it's not all of the sneezing and headaches that I remember so much as the crisp feel, smell and even taste of the leading edge of fall and the time of sowing winter wheat amidst the multi-hued colors of harvest.

We could feel the season changing as we worked. The coming of autumn was in the air all around us and some days, in the sky far above us too. The trill of migrating sandhill cranes returning to the Plains would come down to us from high up in the clear blue.

We would pause in our work to squint our eyes and shade them with our hands, peering upward, looking for the source of the haunting sound. Sometimes we stopped the tractor and piled into the trailer to lie in the corn and watch.

Some have likened autumn to the season of death. In certain respects, if you look only at the maturing of plants and the falling leaves, this is probably so.

Yet, fall days, the gathering of harvest and the spectacle of it all makes this farm boy feel very much alive.

The Blessing of Surplus

Riding a few rounds on the combine is a reminder of how richly blessed we are.

Absent the experience for far too long, I was invited to make a couple of rounds on the combine and the grain cart with a friend while corn harvest was in full swing back in October. The farm boy in me was only too glad for the opportunity and I'm still thinking on it as the season of Thanksgiving approaches.

Out in the field during the bustle of the harvest season, you get to see close-up some of what is real in the world.

The actual work of growing food and producing the sort of wealth that can only come from the soil is not accomplished with Hollywood special effects. Late night know-it-all discussion panels, or the smoke and mirrors and spin-doctoring of politics, or fancy portfolios won't get it done here.

Making grain, fiber or beef is accomplished through mysterious machinations of soil, sunlight, resolve, rain, photosynthesis, horse sense, sweat equity, a lot of luck, and the unswerving constancy of God's providence that makes it all come together somehow.

From the high vantage point of the combine cab, you are witness to the culmination of an awesome process that, through the course of spring and summer and early fall days, transforms nutrients and moisture from the soil and energy from the sun into kernels of grain.

Lore has it that the Indians taught the Pilgrims to drop corn seed into a hole poked in the ground with a stick and to toss in a fish for fertilizer. This acquired skill led to corn harvest sufficient to keep the early Pilgrims alive.

We have come a long way in heading toward the same general end today. Seed that sprouts present-era crops can be precisely metered into the soil 24 rows at a time, the columns of corn spaced 20 inches apart in a mammoth swath of 40 feet in a single pass.

A portrait of harvest viewed from the combine seat is painted in blue-skied, sun-splashed hues of a grand Indian Summer afternoon.

The fruit of labor is spread in vast ocher-leaved legions stretching to the horizon. Tassel-plumed ranks stand at attention, acres and acres in tall, straight columns deployed in dense array to offer up tightly-shucked ears.

The fat of the land mounds in the bins of the harvesting machines. The crop-gobbling headers of the combines devour the golden legions. Roar of engine and thrum of inner rotary workings swiftly shell grain from the cobs and spew fodder, chaff and dust in our wake.

The yield is good, the corn piles high in the grain tank at an astounding rate, and the pace for the carts that are set the task of catching the grain swallowed up and regurgitated by the combines is hectic. A few lost minutes on the part of the grain carts may necessitate a combine stopping with a brimming full grain tank, stalling its gathering process. Grain cart jockeys, fetching loads on the fly, attempt to keep the unloading rate even with the filling as combines roll. Loaded trucks trundle away, churning up turnrow and county road dust, bound to dump their load at a mill where the corn will become a human food product.

The whole of it is an orgy of mechanization and efficiency, a wonderment of bounty, a spirit-lifting experience to observe and photograph and think on.

Yet, watching a harvest being gathered in abundance can also give us pause. We are, even in financially difficult times for the farmlands of this nation, lavishly blessed.

Over a goodly portion of the world, families still farm much as the Pilgrims and Indians did, with sticks and oxen and backbreaking labor. If they are fortunate enough to gather a harvest, what they haul from their fields in a few sacks might be enough to keep them alive, if they are lucky.

Thanks, Lord, for your abundant blessings of the land and its surplus.

Farmyards and Pumpkins

The Carlson family made a tradition of sharing bits of barnyard life and the color of fall with youngsters.

Having worked for a couple of newspapers and a farm magazine in the past, plus free-lancing for other magazines, I have accumulated quite a few slides, photos, negatives and clippings over the years. As hard as it is to get good slides and photos, you hate to throw any of these things away. You never know when you might need a good photographic image again.

Many of my black-and-white negatives and color slides are stored in plastic sleeves clipped in three-ring binders. I never seemed to put together a good filing system for them. I have a general idea of subject matter contained in the ring binders. If I have something in mind for a specific slide, I often have to leaf through several binders seeking what I'm looking for.

In turning the plastic pages, I frequently come across colorful spring and fall images of baby animals, farmsteads and happy kids in pumpkin fields. The color of assorted images and the faces prompt pleasant memories of a local family who made it a tradition to share a bit of rural life with untold numbers of youngsters in the Hereford area.

Back when many of us grew up on the farm, there was traditionally a menagerie of barnyard animals, all sorts of fowl and four-legged critters and maybe even a farm pond. On our own place at Hart, there were two ponds and a wide assortment of ducks, geese, chickens, turkeys, guineas, hogs and cattle.

Modern agriculture and "progress" changed all that, even as my generation was growing up. Farm ponds got filled and farmed. Chicken houses and poultry yards were abandoned and torn down. Fortunately, "modernizing" didn't erase every trace of barnyard heritage hereabouts.

The late Lawrence Carlson and his wife Betty Jo never modernized so much that they didn't keep barnyard critters for a good many years at their place just south and west of Milo Center, and later, their son Roy carried on the tradition of hospitality to youngsters in his pumpkin fields.

Lawrence's and Betty Jo's home place was within reasonable driving distance of local schools, so a field trip by bus or van could be mounted easily.

Because of their willingness to share it in a show-and-tell fashion, the Carlson place became a virtual cornucopia of fun, excitement and education for hosts of Hereford kindergarten kids who are adults now.

Today, lots of kids, and adults for that matter, have no idea where eggs or milk or meat come from. In its heyday, the Carlson place at least gave a lot of delighted youngsters a happy clue.

A spring field trip to the Carlsons generally would allow inquisitive kindergartners to see crowing roosters, clucking hens and peeping chicks, geese and goslings, and ducks and ducklings. Out in the lot by the barn, there were usually some baby calves, a couple of husky draft horses and maybe even a colt to look at. Some of the kids might get to help gather a few eggs from hiding places within the hay. Everybody learned that the old knob-nosed gander with flailing wings could be a testy sort and that baby chicks generally stuck close to Mama when five-year-olds were on the loose.

What did kids learn from all of this? That farm animals are real and some nice folks were happy to show them so. For a few, this may have been their only exposure to live farm animals.

Fall came to be quite an event at the Carlson place. On a few occasions, Lawrence hitched his team of draft horses — the ones he used to plow the garden and the orchard — to a wagon and gave an assemblage of lucky youngsters a real old-fashioned hay ride.

Come October, there were the pumpkins. Roy grew them commercially for several years and for little folks, the pumpkin acreage at the Carlson farm became a place to seek their own colorful fall prize.

Youngsters from kindergarten and elementary classes in Hereford and Vega flocked to the Carlson place to roam orange-beaded fields in search of perfect pumpkins that were just their size.

Huffing and puffing, short-legged youngsters would stagger from the field under the weight of brilliant prizes they had chosen for themselves.

The orbs may have been orange, but they and the happy times they fostered were pure fall gold for youngsters and for those who shared with them.

Fall Orange

There is universal appeal in a crisp fall day and a field of colorful pumpkins.

Fall is brightened by a truly American icon—the deep golden orange of pumpkins. Even city folk, usually standoffish when it comes to anything to do with a farm, are strangely drawn to the colorfully rural images of "frost on the punkin' and fodder in the shock."

What is so universally appealing about fall and pumpkins? They have been attractive to man throughout history. Although it is uncertain where the pumpkin originated, history notes the value of the mystical powers of the pumpkin in ancient China. The first pumpkin pie was recorded to be baked by primitive means in the United Kingdom. Pumpkin was already a dietary staple before Plymouth Rock, cultivated by Native American tribes and eaten roasted, boiled and stewed. At the first Thanksgiving feast in 1621, pumpkins—named for the medieval European squash "pompion" and for the Greek "pepon," meaning "cooked by the sun"—were on the menu along with turkey and corn.

Yankee ingenuity led to a brew made from fermented pumpkins and persimmons flavored with maple sugar.

Pumpkins are especially thought of in their decorative role. Jack o'lanterns are generally credited to early Irish settlers. Folklore holds that a stingy drunkard named Jack was given a jack o'lantern by the devil as a feeble light and sent to roam the earth in search of a place to rest. Other folk tales trace the origin of jack o'lanterns to the Druids or to early England.

It was believed that the eerie light cast by hollowed-out, carved, lighted pumpkins would ward off evil spirits. There is nothing too evil-spirited in the quest by children and adults for the perfect jack o'lantern pumpkin.

For years, Roy and Shirley Carlson grew several acres of commercial pumpkins out at Milo Center. Roy would plant carving and pie-variety pumpkins and even some decorative miniatures.

Each fall the Carlsons would treat classes of local school youngsters to a trip to their pumpkin patch. The kids got to roam and pick out their own perfect pumpkin.

Peddlers would buy pumpkins right out of the field. Shirley sold pumpkins out of their front yard alongside Highway 385. Sales were self-service on the honor system. You could pick out a pumpkin from scores of them spread on the ground and atop a flatbed trailer or grain truck, then leave your money in a can or box if nobody was around. Evidently, the honor system worked reasonably well. Shirley made grocery money and lots of folks got to load up on orange orbs of fall. Fresh pumpkin pie didn't last long around Shirley's house with three boys and Roy all going after it.

Hailstorms and diseases cut down on the pumpkin planting on the Carlson spread. Roy sometimes still grows a small patch and even tried a novel white variety.

Local carrot man Larry Malamen also diversifies his orange products by planting a small patch of pumpkins each year. Somebody has to keep a few pumpkins growing locally.

Pumpkin growing goes way back in Floyd County, where B.A. "Slim" Robertson started growing them. Slim was known as "the pumpkin man." He started out with ten acres and added more as demand grew. He at first sold his crop at roadside, later shipping truckloads to market. Slim became a Floyd County legend after he received a letter addressed simply to "the pumpkin patch southwest of Floydada."

They take their pumpkin growing seriously at Floydada, proclaiming themselves "Punkin' Capital of the U.S.A." They stage a big punkin' festival each fall that draws lots of folks. Over half of all the pumpkins grown in Texas are produced in Floyd County.

Today you can get pumpkins from miniatures a couple of inches around through pie-sized, and on up to mammoth orbs. The world's largest pumpkin weighed over 750 pounds.

Joe Ike Clay, down at Flomot, is one of those sand-country farmers who is always scratching for another way to make a little income with something besides cotton and goober peas. Years ago Joe Ike decided to grow some giant pumpkins that would make awesome jack-o'-lanterns.

The pumpkins grew wonderfully on Motley County's sandy soil and colored-up rich reddish-orange.

Come harvest time, Joe Ike wrestled a few 200-pound pumpkins onto a trailer in the field and a light suddenly came on in his *cabeza*.

To grow a whopper punkin'
would really be sumthin.'
But, whopper punkins, he wudda' never growed
...If he had knowed
....They was such a pain in the...back...to load!

Inside a White Cow

At times when the weather turns the worst Plains folk are at their neighborly best.

Just before Palm Sunday—in the spring supposedly—the man had sold a few calves at the Tulia auction. Unloading the calves, waiting for them to sell and getting the paperwork in order took longer than he had figured on, but he got them sold. With the trailer rattling behind his pickup, he struck out across country, making for home.

Despite what the calendar and the whimsical pictures of sunshine-splashed Easter fashion in the catalogs were saying about spring, the powers that form the weather on the Plains were having none of it.

A gathering haze of blue in the north had sent low clouds scudding from horizon to horizon as the day progressed. The clouds were flush with a dark shade of foreboding.

The man watched the weather forming and wished he had gotten on the road hours earlier, and that he had more to keep him warm than a denim jacket and a Stetson hat. He made a mental note to stuff a "just-in-case" pair of insulated coveralls in the space behind the pickup seat where he would have them next time.

Snowflakes filtered down from a cold sky, at first large and fluffy and wet. Thumping windshield wipers swished them away as they melted against the defroster-warmed windshield.

The frigid north wind gathered force at sundown and a dark pall of clouds drew the curtains over what might have otherwise been another glorious sunset.

The fast-moving norther smothered the daylight, its bluster propelling snow in a slanting, blinding curtain.

Wind-driven snow was falling so heavily against the beam of the headlights that it seemed a solid sheet. The motion of the descending snowflakes skewed his senses if he looked at them for long. Better to concentrate on the road. He knew the blacktop was there beneath the pickup tires, but it was hard to make out anything resembling a pavement.

He turned south at the Lakeview Gin, just able to make out the dim shape of the old schoolhouse before the corner, and did a little better going away from the wind with the snowflakes racing outward from the windshield. In only a few miles, he had to turn westward on his journey again. Once more, the snow was sheeting across the road before him, hurled by a full-blown gale.

He kept a light foot on the gas pedal, the pickup creeping along. He was still able to see a patch of road now and again. The places where the road ran parallel to smooth-plowed fields were the worst, the snow roiling across the roadway in a great sight-robbing slick. He had heard it many times—had made the comment himself about a room or the night being darker than the inside of a black cow. He thought to himself as he clutched the steering wheel and stared hard at the road that this must be what it was like to be inside a white one.—As far as he was concerned, not being able to see in all of this stuff wasn't any better than stumbling around in the pitch black.

The defroster roared in protest against the frigid howling of the wind outside the pickup cab. Snow was piling up and he was worried that he would be spending the night stalled out here on the roadside.

A swirling cloud of powder enveloped the pickup. Inching through, he could just make out the pale-blue-but-hopeful haze of a yard light somewhere up ahead.

The last two miles were near-impossible. By the time he reached that light, he was shaking from nerves as much as cold. Yet, a yellow shaft of light beamed invitingly through the window of a farmhouse served by the blue security light.

He shoved his way out of the pickup, wallowed through a snow drift at the edge of the front porch and managed to find his way to the farmhouse door. His frantic pounding brought a quick response.

Flinging the door open wide, a weathered resident called out, "Come in here and kick your boots off, feller, it's not fit out for man or beast."

The door closed snugly behind him and he was out of the teeth of the storm. He left his boots on the rug at the door. He was invited into the warm, bright kitchen where they were making pancakes and eggs for supper. They sat him down at the table, put a plate with a steaming stack in front of him and poured him hot coffee. The people who lived here understood what it was to be caught in such weather.

They dined, they visited, they made him comfortable and dry, and bunked him for the night, the best they could and in the morning they fed him again.

The storm blew itself out in the night. The new day dawned clear, the crystalline snow sparkling in the cold, sharp, sun-spangled air. Late in the morning, the farm folks fired-up their dual-wheeled diesel tractor that had been plugged into a block warmer all night. They didn't know if it would start in the cold. The engine moaned and growled before kicking over, then caught and whitish smoke spewed out the exhaust pipe. They let the rig warm up a long time. Finally, they pulled the tractor around the front of his pickup, hitched onto it with a chain, and gave him a pull the last half-mile down to the north-south highway that hadn't filled with drifts. It was clear-enough for him to travel.

The man from the farmhouse who knew a neighbor when he saw one shook hands, wished him a safe journey and sent him on his way.

As he made good progress on his way home, the man who sold the calves had his mind full of a truth he had come to understand and appreciate.

In the Plains, when the weather is at its worst, prairie people are often at their best.

What is it With Mamas?

They shape and mold and fill our lives while doing all sorts of weird and unexplainable things.

What is it with Mamas? You spend roughly the first half of your life arguing endlessly with them. They aren't up to speed on so many things. They are dense and slow, contrary and don't know how to be "cool."

All-knowing youth find them silly, sentimental, stick-in-the-mud sorts. They spoil our "fun," not letting us stay out all night to bay at the moon and raise hell. Mamas embarrass us no end, acting "dumb" in front of our friends. They probably emerged from the womb as adults. They are all of the time coming up with stupid remarks...*Come in out of the rain and pour that water out of our boot if we have sense enough to read the directions on the heel...Take our coat along, it's snowing...Carry our socks and underwear to the laundry...Finish our homework before we go outside...Feed the dog, the cat, the hogs, the horses...*

Don't slouch...Take some responsibility...Work is good for you...Be polite...Play nice...Refill the ice trays...Wash your dishes...Fold your laundry and put it away...Clean your room...Don't put beans in your ears...Take a bath—whether you think you need it or not...Be home before dark...Don't pull your sister's hair, or poke your kid brother in the eye...Call when you get there...Say yes ma'am, yes sir, please and thank you.

Nobody who comes up with this sort of stuff could ever have been a kid, could they?

They have eyes in the backs of their heads. When we fall quiet, they always know we are up to something—and exactly what kind of mischief we're about to get into.

Now, trying to raise know-it-alls of our own, we seek them out. They are gurus of child-rearing. We need their sound advice. We ask them to share gems of wisdom and, they do.

Their secrets are so simple and effective. Be polite. Play nice. Wash our dishes. Tote our socks and underwear. Refill the ice trays. Don't put beans in our ears. Be responsible. Sounds vaguely familiar. Somebody surely should have told us these secrets long before now.

What is it with Mamas?

They never sleep. They hear our fevered stirring, brought on in the night by colds and flu and tummy aches, ouchies and itchies, bumps and bruises, hurts of body and soul, real or imagined. They come to us when we call out, whether we are just down the hall or halfway across the heartland.

They sponge our heated brow, smooth back our tousled hair, bring soothing comfort, cough medicine, 7-Up, chicken soup, healing with their hands, their voices and their hearts—giving constantly from their hearts, even as we are breaking them.

Forever awake, they listen for reassurance that we are snuggled in our beds, wayward hooligans safely home.

What is it with Mamas?

They scent and flavor our lives. Smells of talcum and baby oil, bleach and laundry soap, hot irons, stinky home perms, furniture polish, scouring powder, dishwater, sewing machine oil, house paint, hand lotion, hair spray, fingernail polish, bubble bath, perfume.

Dashes of cinnamon and sugar and nutmeg, vanilla and ginger, maple and chocolate, powdered and brown sugar. Sprinkled salt and pepper. Sage and poultry seasoning. Blotches of flour and corn meal.

Through back-aching, knee-buckling labor, they prepare a hundred flawless Thanksgiving and Christmas, New Year's and Easter feasts that make our mouths water. Nothing tastes quite so good as Mom's cooking.

Forever they say that they don't mind when we come through the front door right at mealtime with unexpected extras in tow to crowd their too-small kitchens. It is no trouble, they say with smiles. They are diplomatic liars—smooth as silk.

What is it with Mamas?

Their hands deliver much: Bread, kneaded and rolled and fresh-baked; patches sewed on the seat of jeans; a few well-aimed swats placed there as well; band-aids for cut fingers and scraped knees. Their hand labor tells us, without words, that they love us.

They give pies and patience, cookies and consolation, donuts and discipline, compassion, relief, reason, religion, openness and orange slice cake—even if the batter *is* hard to stir.

They work all day in the field or the office and still put food on the table with lightning speed. They can fry meat and make flawless gravy, sprinkling in just the right amount of flour and an exact quantity of milk, though it is poured straight from the jug with nary a measuring spoon.

What is it with Mamas?

We thought that they nagged so severely they could never have been kids. Now when we get cross with ours, Mamas ask, "Don't you remember how it was when you were a kid?"

They do. Their memories are as sharp as their sewing scissors. They can recall first steps, fine curls, cuddly toys, puppy dogs, delighted Christmas morning faces, great report cards, slumber parties, birthdays, prom nights, high school graduation, bringing home that special boy or girl to meet them.

Those sharp memories have some fuzzy edges. They forget pain and hardships endured for us, recall, only vaguely, arguments that came about because of our ornery bullheadedness. They knew, at times, that our actions were going to bring us grief, but the best thing that they could do was to let us live life and suffer the consequences of our actions. They did. Hard as it was for them, they let us fall a few times, so that we would be stronger when we got back up.

They have every right to say, "I told you so," a few million times, but mostly, they don't.

What is it with Mamas?

Character flaw, I guess. Thank God.

Easter is for...

Sunrise and second chances...Pastel dresses, colored eggs, joys for little and big kids.

Easter is for...

Being dragged by the arm off to town on a perfectly good day, when the weather says "Let's play outside," but instead we have to stand around in stores and try on stuff. There's nothing wrong with the clothes that we have. Almost everything we are coerced into trying on is just too dandy to wear. We cram our feet into new, tight, shiny shoes that are supposed to be just the cat's pajamas and hear endlessly how "cute" the whole getup is.

Easter is for...

Coloring eggs. Maybe this is to make up for having to go shopping. We get to wear comfortable "old clothes" for this job of hard-boiling eggs and dipping them in cups of egg dye to create color for the season.

The most hard-boiled eggs you ever saw anyone eat in a sitting was three, but we have to make up at least a couple dozen colored eggs to help out the hard-working Easter bunny. It's lots more fun than shopping, dipping the eggs in the dye, mixing and creating colors, and dusting the eggs with sparkles.

Easter is for...

The debut of the spring look at church. Girls have new shoes and hats, purses and pastel-colored dresses and white gloves. The gloves have no earthly purpose, except to lug around and get dirty and to be put in and taken out of the new purse. One of the gloves will invariably be lost somewhere between church and home.

All of this fashion stuff was bought on the shopping trip. The girls all dress to the teeth in the latest spring fashions, but the hep designers and chic clothing stores do not take into account the reality of spring in the Texas High Plains. Easter Sunday is likely to be cold and windy. Then the girls don the latest and most fashionable and pull on overcoats that smother the fashion statement for the practicality of warmth.

A viselike grip on the Easter bonnets will be necessary in the face of stout spring wind, an ever-present part of Easter Sunday in the Panhandle.

Easter is for...

Sunrise and second chances. Wondering at dawn and dogwood, an empty tomb and full heart, lilies and life, failings and forgiveness. Watching a bare and somber splintered wooden cross at the front of the church bloom as it is adorned with flowers placed upon it by children. Feeling the triumph of hope.

Easter is for...

Photo opportunities. Nobody gets washed-behind-the-ears spiffed-up that often. When a day like Easter Sunday comes along, it is going to be documented. Hapless victims get shoved in front of the living room curtains, the blooming bushes out back, pots of fragrant lilies and told to stand still and look nice. New shirts and jackets, ties and dresses itch and bind and irritate and make us fidget. Mom and Uncle Homer and Aunt Florena and Dad and Grandpa and even cousins whose names you can't remember fiddle with their cameras, setting the timer, dashing to get in the frame, getting backsided when they are too slow, or blinded when the flash goes off in their face as they stoop to see why it didn't go off while they waited among the crowd of photo subjects.

They snap pictures endlessly and ooh and aah over how pretty and handsome we all look through their viewfinder. They seem always to want "just one more picture," though it is getting to be dinner-thirty and we can smell fried chicken and imagine fresh-mashed potatoes heaped with white gravy on our plates out in the kitchen. It is hard for amateur photographers to get "still" shots.

Easter is for...

Egg hunts. After fried chicken and ham, roast beef and turkey, potatoes and gravy and biscuits and other niceties are devoured in the wake of photo opportunities, there comes a mid-afternoon time when youngsters are shooshed to a back room and the older set hauls cartons of boiled eggs and sacks of colorful candies to the closest winter wheat patch. Red and orange and yellow and purple and white and pink prizes are "hidden" amongst lush green wheat. The kids get word that it's time to find eggs. You never saw a Mom drag a kid off to the mall any faster than those youngsters haul everybody to the wheat patch. Grown-ups required more than 30 minutes to hide all of those eggs. Little basket-toting egg hunters sweep the area and vacuum up the colorful prizes in a couple of minutes.

The egg hunters taste their find. Marshmallow candy eggs, malted "robin eggs" and jellybeans, chocolate eggs with soft centers, and foil-wrapped chocolate bunnies, all warmed to a squishy consistency by the sun on the wheat field.

Egg hunters share their prizes with grandparents, who are just big kids.—Easter is for youngsters of all ages to smear chocolate bunnies and eggs and marshmallows and such all over their delighted faces.

A Few Daddyisms

Time imparts age to wine, patina to wood, mellowness to memories, and appreciation of things Dad said and did.

A few of the fatherly comments that we have heard over the years, concerning everyday events, and making your way in life:

- ✦ "Always take care of first things first...God and family come first."
- ✦ "You're only as good as your word."
- ✦ "The best thing that a man can give his kids is his time."
- ✦ "Take care of the land and it will take care of you."
- ✦ "You can't grow a crop if you're doing all of your farming from behind a pickup windshield."
- ✦ "Farming so that the place looks pretty is okay, but you can do such a pretty job of farming that it will break you."
- ✦ "Can't raise much of anything if you don't raise a little sweat."
- ✦ "Don't be in such a hurry to pull out in traffic that you don't stop and look both ways. We've sure got a lot more time than we have money."
- ✦ "Drive like hell and you'll get there."
- ✦ "Listening to that fellow talk for about half-a-day is like riding over 90 miles of bad road."
- ✦ "If you are going to pull in double harness, don't be kicking over the traces."
- ✦ "Your good name is worth a lot more than money."
- ✦ "A hog's in no hurry. All that he has to do is eat and sleep."
- ✦ "Don't worry about it. How much difference is it going to make a hundred years from now?"
- ✦ "You don't have to be in such a rush to finish. Let's sit down here and rest a minute. It will still be there."
- ✦ "Don't think that you're too good to wash dishes or do laundry."
- ✦ "Pick that nail up out of the road and save some poor fellow the price of a flat."
- ✦ "Pull the dipstick on that thing and see if there's any oil in it.—Oil's cheaper than bearings."

- "Look how well that hoe handle fits your hand."
- "Some of us have already put in half a day's work before some of us got out of bed."

When we were all flash and dash and wise beyond our years—we thought—Dads plodded along mundanely. They didn't do things in the all-fired hurry that half-cocked youth demanded. They weren't sold on sparkle over substance.

Didn't matter how stylishly you wielded the hoe if the weeds were still standing. Didn't make any difference if the hog farmers going by the textbook were turning out three sets of top hogs a year on expensive "hot" feed, while you were getting only two on homegrown corn. Your hogs took longer but the feed was cheap and the bottom line came out in the black. Didn't matter what kind of sporty rigs everybody else was driving. Ours might not be flashy, but it was paid for. Didn't matter if you didn't make varsity, long as you did your best, played hard and clean and had fun. Didn't matter if you made some honest mistakes along the way, it was how you learned.

What does matter is loving and helping one another, getting along, giving respect, sharing what you have, always paying your bills,—paying them as-you-go if you can—a few laughs along the way, a good steak, a nap on Sunday afternoon, never being so busy that you can't appreciate those around you or take the time to watch the pheasants court, the coyotes hunt, the geese fly into the corn field, or pull up your plow and go around the mallard nest at the bottom end of the field.

We thought, years ago, that the old man was just too tight to spring for new nails at the lumberyard. When he was rebuilding something, he would pull nails, straighten them against the concrete or a piece of wood with a hammer, save them and drive them again when he needed them.

What was it that came over us when we were re-working the back yard fence? We noticed that a lot of the nails that we pulled didn't look bad, so we tossed them in a can. When we put up new boards, we straightened the old nails with rapid taps of the hammer as we rolled them over against the fence posts and used them again. They were perfectly good. I really don't think it made the boards any difference whether the nails were new or not.

Time imparts age to wine, patina to wood, mellowness to memories—and gradually, appreciation of the wisdom of a lot of those "dumb" things that our Daddies said and did through the years.

Country Christmas Eve

Small though you are in the scheme of the universe, twinkling Christmas couriers bring a message to you.

The layer of ice covering the stock tank yields to steady blows of the axe that send glistening crystalline chips and showers of spray flying in all directions.

Some of the big outfits have floating heaters on their tanks that make this job unnecessary. Ah well, the axe wields easily on this day, its bit gnawing a ragged opening. Shoving some of the chunks out of the way with the head of the axe frees up the underlying water.

Cattle that have waited impatiently edge up to the water and slurp noisily. They have been on the wheat all day, and made the long, loping walk back to water in a fittingly serene manner.

The western sky is bathed in the crimson rays of the setting sun as you move to the south side of the barn.

Tossing the fork up on the flatbed trailer, you scramble up the side onto it. The trailer is piled high with ear corn gathered from fallen stalks the combine missed and the eight rows that were the big roasting ear patch.

Shoving the fork into the mound of ochre shucks with your foot, you hurl cascades of corn to the squealing hogs. Quickly the squealing gives way to rustling and steady chomping. The hogs stand on the ends of the ears of corn, nimbly peel back the shucks and devour the grain. There is much smacking and contented grunting.

Taking the bucket from the fence, you retrace your steps to the stock tank, pushing the floating ice aside with the edge of the bucket, then dipping deeply. Water sloshes over the rim of the bucket as you walk back towards the hog pen, arm outstretched for balance.

Atop the fence panel you tilt the bucket, sending a cascade of water into the trough. By the time that you are halfway to the stock tank again, your fingers are numb from the cold. A second bucket of water, then a third, is also dumped into the trough. As you drape the bucket over the fence post where it will be handy for tomorrow, contentment is coming to you, too.

You stop by the horse pen. The old mare, already fed, gives a friendly nicker...Maybe a little more hay wouldn't hurt...Not tonight, anyway. Breaking open a new haygrazer bale, you throw half of it across the fence. Horses are always hungry.

Leaning on the fence to talk to the horse and rub her flanks, there is time to take everything in as the first of the evening stars begin to twinkle even as the last light of day rapidly retreats. Looking into the December night, you realize just how fitting an old barn, a bale of hay and a handful of livestock truly are on this night.

The chores are finished. Despite the mounting chill of the evening, there is no rush to get back to the house. In the fading light, you pause at the edge of the lot to look over things you love. The lush wheat field is only a dark splotch, belying the greenery that spells good fare for the cattle.

Leaves and shucks from the harvested corn and maize fields rustle in the breeze that is rising with the evening. The grain crops may not have been all that was hoped for, but they were not bad, considering the year. Dry times and curled leaves through part of the summer gave way to hope when unexpected rains came in July. Even the threat of early snow passed and the crop remained standing until the combine gathered it. Maybe, with another break or two from the weather, the crops would have turned out better. We still have this piece of land and we're together. We're not wanting for a whole lot, even if the grain bins aren't brimming. We have a roof over our heads, food on the table, all of the best things our Maker can bestow and the freedom to enjoy them.

Somewhere off in the sorghum stubble, a cock pheasant gives his hoarse cackle and the sound of wind whistling through the wings of ducks can be heard as they pass overhead on their way to feed in the corn field.

Hunkered within your down jacket and coveralls, hands in your pockets, you ponder descending night, pierced by a growing profusion of sparkling constellations. They are a source of unending wonder, these pulsating lanterns of the heavens.

Who can number the stars on this night? They are so incredibly bright in the cold, clear sky. Your breath drifts upward in silvery puffs against the chill.

A shiver of delight comes. Small though you are in the grand universe, you are greeted by the couriers of Christmas. Standing in the farmyard beneath the vast, star-flecked sky, you understand the overwhelming awe that the shepherds must have felt when angels appeared amidst the starry night to proclaim the first message of Christmas to simple folk tending their stock, long years ago.

The good feeling is alive when you move toward the light pouring from the window.

The warmth from the kitchen fogs your glasses as you step onto the back porch, shed the coveralls, wriggle out of the jacket and kick off your boots.

You can already smell the tree. Without looking, you know it is there, its glittering lights and tinsel as bright in your mind as they are in the living room down the hall.

The kitchen is filled with the odors of freshly-baked bread and cakes, cinnamon and sugar and pecans, roasting turkey and giblets going at a slow boil—all the trimmings of a holiday that say that you are home again.

Dad is in his chair at the kitchen table, already out of his insulated coveralls and thawing the edge off the chill of a day's work with steaming coffee.

Mom and the girls are scurrying around the crowded kitchen, peeling potatoes, sprinkling seasonings, making the crucial taste tests as they tend the pots and pans that will yield tonight's supper and tomorrow's feast.

You snatch a biscuit off the top of the stove and dodge the mild scolding that ensues as you go to wash up.

By now, it's not the heat from Mom's hard-working oven that is warming you.

It is Christmas Eve in the farm country. Somehow, Bethlehem doesn't seem that far away.

The Messenger

Was it just a cold combiner
   Talking to them on that day,
Of a great event in Bethlehem
   Long ago and far away?

Golden days of autumn
   Had given way to winter's blast
Harvest dragged into December,
   'Ere they gathered in the last.

A lot of hard-luck farmers
   Had struggled since last June,
Fighting drought and hail and bugs
   And then, winter's ice had come too soon.

Now with the crop's final gathering
   To the elevator office they did come
To sit by the fire, drink coffee,
   And tally this harvest's dismal sum.

They bemoaned the crop's shortcomings,
   They drank of scalding brew
And the mood, it was in general
   Most miserably forlorn, it's true.

A beat-up old truck clattered
   Upon that elevator's scales,
Its driver ducked in the office door,
   Likely with another hard-luck tale.

This tall, cover-alled amigo
Was a stranger nobody knew
   —Probably just another member
Of some froze-out harvest crew.

He poured himself a steaming cup,
    Then pulled up a cow cake sack,
He perched on it, leaned on the wall,
    And the conversation, it fell slack.

This stranger, he sure was different,
    Than any they had met to now,
His face all peaceful, friendly, smiling,
    —Downright radiant, somehow.

"Harvest's been a tough one
    "Now, folks, I'm here to tell,
That things, they aren't all that bad,
    In fact, they are downright well."

This speaker had the attention
    Of counter-sitters and scalemen, too,
They figured this combiner had a line,
    Now, just what was it that he knew?

The stranger, he launched into a tale
    That drove out doubts and frets,
A story of Christmas magic,
    That they're still repeating, yet.

He spoke of stars high in the heavens
    Showering twinkling, benevolent light,
Down on anxious shepherds
    Standing watch, shivering with fright.

He told how the skies were a spectacle
    Upon that most wondrous eve,
Sights and sounds and happenings
    To celebrate the world's reprieve.

He said there came a message
    From a sweet-voiced heavenly throng,
Glad tidings of peace upon the earth
    Were the words of their joyous song.

Angels assured frightened shepherds
    That they need not have any fear,
And gifted them with a Noel message
    Of glad tidings and good cheer.

The stranger recollected how angels
    Bid shepherds, come see a newborn King,
Born in a lowly Bethlehem stable,
    Man's salvation was His gift to bring.

He told how God's own son was born
    Though not in a palace grand,
The light of the world was kindled
    Among livestock and folks of the land.

"The Good Shepherd came to Earth,
    To show the straight and narrow way,
He was born beside ox, ass and lamb,
    And swaddled upon their hay.

"The Savior came to a common walk
    Amongst stockmen and farmers, too,
Preaching of herding, plowing, reaping,
    And sowing good seed that would yield true.

"He could have come to lofty places
    Amidst pageantry great and grand,
Instead, he came to common folk,
    Who worked hard with their hands.

"So, my poor discouraged, farmers,
    Don't you sit here feeling glum,
For Christmas Day is drawing nigh,
    And to country folk, He did come.

"In the eons since the very first
    Celebration of His holy birth,
Not all that very much has changed,
    We still rejoice in Him on Earth.

"Worry not o'er your harvest,
    Nor fickle markets that may seem poor,
For the labors that you do down here
    Bring you nearer to Heaven's door.

"Now lay ye down your burdens,
    Your worries and your cares,
Be of help to one another,
    And the great glad tidings share."

The stranger smiled, put down his cup,
    Then made right for the door
The dark mood that once held the room
    Now existed there no more.

The stranger piled into his truck
    And cranked it up just right,
This Noel messenger spoke once more,
    Then was gone in a flash of light.

Was it combiner or Christmas angel
    Bringing a message of good cheer?
None of them could rightly say,
    But his words, they still ring clear:

"Keep ever the faith, you farmers,
    Stockmen and people of the land,
Your Heavenly Father knows your needs,
    And He holds you in His hand.

"The tidings I bring are not so changed
    Even in this time and day,
From those I brought to shepherds
    Long years ago and far away.

"Joy be yours in this season,
    For in answer to prayers that you say,
Unto you comes the greatest gift,
    Christ, the Lord, on Christmas Day."

The Cowboy Camp

You never know just who will be
calling on your hospitality.

Way out upon the plains land
   Where the lonesome wind does blow,
A crude cow camp had been pitched
   Around a prairie-coal fire's glow.

The horses of the remuda
   On a long static line were tethered,
They stamped and whinnied and snorted
   After another long day weathered.

Around the camp were scattered
   Trail-worn saddles and bedrolls, too,
Out in the open was sleeping quarters
   For this winter cowherd crew.

A splintered old chuckwagon
   Had been unhitched at this site,
The cook, he was a-workin' hard
   To get the cowhands fed tonight.

In Dutch ovens buried 'midst the coals,
   Sourdough biscuits were a-makin',
And he was tryin' to rustle up
   Some gritty beans and bacon.

He was boilin' up some 'taters,
   He had whacked 'em up some onion,
And since he had all the makins'
   There was vinegar pie a-comin'.

Most any other workin' day
  All this effort would make him grumble,
But tonight the boys would get plenty,
  Even if the eats was humble.

Old Cooky, he was doin' his best
  To be good to the crew,
He kept the coffee pot on the fire,
  So they'd have plenty of dark, hot brew.

They were far out on the trail this night,
  Away from home, dear ones, good cheer,
Not a top hand amongst 'em even knew
  What day it was out here.

The cowboys sprawled around the fire
  A-waitin' for their fare.
They sipped bitter coffee from steaming cups
  And rolled collars against chill air.

The roof o'er their heads upon this night,
  Was a sparkling array of wonder,
Ten million stars shone clear and bright
  Glinting away up yonder.

Don't think they'd ever seen a night,
  When the stars was any clearer,
You coulda' reached out and grabbed a few
  If they was any nearer.

From away out on the prairie vast,
  There came a strong clear voice,
"Hello the camp, you cowhands there,
  Tis a night we should rejoice.

"Hello the camp, I'm ridin' in,
    And meanin' you no harm,
So stay your hands, don't fret a'tall,
    You've no cause for alarm."

Out of the darkness materialized,
    A scene most astonishing,
A tall rider on a big white hoss
    Where before they hadn't seen a thing.

The rider and his prancing mount
    Had a look right shiny to see.
That stranger, he rode tall and proud
    All confident and carefree.

"Evenin' gents," the stranger called,
    "I could smell your supper cookin,'
And figured you could stand company,
    The way you boys was lookin'."

"Light and hitch," old cook called out,
    "Yo're welcome as you can be,
Sit a spell, have vittles with us,
    No need ridin' 'round empty."

The stranger spoke his heartfelt thanks,
    Tied his horse, flopped his saddle down,
Pulled up a seat next to the fire,
    And Cooky passed tin plates around.

"Now, boys," said the rider, "This is right kind
    To share your meal with me,
To get square for this neighboring,
I'll tell you an age-old story.

"I know how cowpokes, they don't hold
    Too much with herding sheep,
But it was boys a lot like you
    The angels roused from sleep...

"Upon this very night, you see,
    Just a spell of years ago,
Angels made herdsmen just like you
    The very first to know...

"That God's own son was come to earth
    On that first Christmas night,
He came down here to live with us
    And show us what was right...

"I figure cowboys are not too far
    From those shepherd boys of old,
They kept watch over critters, too,
    In the nights so dark and cold...

"So I say to all of you cowpokes,
    Heed this message of good cheer,
For the word of the first Christmas
    Has been brought down to you here."

The astonished cowboys all blurted out,
    " Who are you man, do tell,
To ride in here amongst us,
    With word of the first Noel?"

The visitor rose up and caught his hoss,
    And throwed the saddle on,
Before they could even say a word,
    He was saddled, ready to be gone.

" I thank you, boys, for sharing
   Your fine plains hospitality."
He tipped his hat, and with a nod,
    Said, " Gabe's what folks call me...

" I'd best be gone, the night is long
    And I've other camps to call on."
  He wheeled his hoss, slapped reins and boss,
    In that instant...they was gone...

"Well, I'll declare," the old cook hollered,
  " Was glad tidin's old Gabe brung us,
I ask you boys, who wudda' thought
    An angel would ride among us?"

When at last they rolled-in for the night,
   Their hearts were filled with wonder,
At the Christmas gift they had received
   On the lonesome plains out yonder.

Keep it Simple, Stupid

A fallen branch told me:
We make Christmas harder than it ought to be.

"I just hate to see 'it' coming any more," the grandmotherly lady sighed as we exchanged greetings and steered our shopping carts to pass side-by-side in the narrow aisle the giant retailer had left between piled-high wrapping paper on one side and assorted ornaments and varied junk on the other.

Ever shopping-wary, and now shopping-weary, I knew the overwhelmed feeling she was describing. Here came the holiday season, bearing down like a runaway train. She was probably already in frenzied planning and preparation for what she hoped would be a memorable blowout for the family. The tasks that lay before her, whether real or imagined, must be completed before Christmas. She was already feeling the pressure.

We hadn't even laid in the turkey for Thanksgiving at our house yet, and here we were, elbowing our way through the consumer mayhem of it all. We were trapped in shopping hell, surrounded by mountains of tin and tinsel, bulbs and bows, fake renditions of pine and fir, electric-driven animation of elves and Santas and snowmen, the ceaseless bombardment of tinny music from figurines.

Windup and battery-driven jangles mixed ill with the "music" blaring over the public address system. The casual shopper was quickly rendered deaf, or numb, or both, by what I suppose was intended to soothe and put customers in a holiday spirit of spending.

I watched young parents drag their small, gawking child through this mass of confusion. He seemed as stupefied by it all as I was.

What kind of impression of Christmas, what sort of wide-eyed wonder at the season was a kiddo to draw from all of this?

When had Christmas, the childhood favorite season, been reduced to an "it?" When had Christmas become something to be dreaded, rather than anxiously anticipated?

We bumped and jostled, dodged and weaved, fought and clawed our way through the crowds. The store was so congested that overeager cart-pushers were clipping my heels in their zeal to get to the next deal. At long last we finished the foray, then ran for home.

I wondered at what was wrong with this picture on the drive back to small town civilization.

Back home and unloaded, I made a trip to the alley to dispose of some of the day's accumulated trash.

The wind of the previous November evening had ripped a heavy upper branch from one of the blue-needled cedar trees flanking the south side of the alley. I like that row of evergreens. They dampen the road noise and give us a little privacy on the back 40. They are a haven for colorful birds from mourning doves to bluejays. They ease the burn of the southerly sun in the summer and buffer the blasts of fitful winds in the spring.

The soft-needled uppermost parts of the wounded branch hung by a sliver of bark, wedged between the trunk and other trees. A boisterous breeze had wreaked its havoc in the night, when the likelihood of anyone walking beneath the tree was remote. The broken branch was nearly as big-around as a man's leg. Had it fallen on someone's *cabeza*, it would surely have inflicted a substantial *el cabong*.

I got a saw and big pruning loppers to take this dangling hazard down before it could nail the neighbor lady.

A few minutes of pushing the saw heated me up, despite the brisk temperature. The branch broke free and crashed to the ground. I wrestled it around where I could work it down to manageable size. I used the loppers to whack off all of the branches that I could get its jaws around.

Some flexes of the wooden handles, some gashes by the business end of the tool, and fresh, tacky, skin-tarring sap was oozing. The odor from the work was familiar—that of Christmases years back, when trees were real and shopping malls weren't.

A noseful of this and I thought about how Dad used to lug in a soft-needled Christmas tree that would stand in the hole in the middle of an old implement flywheel, that was itself placed in the bottom end of a steel barrel that served as a water pan. The tree, and Christmas itself, were real enough then.

I thought about the time that Pancho used tree branches much like I was lopping off to fashion a stable for the church nativity scene, and how we used the fresh, sweet-smelling greenery left from his work to cover the stable roof.

Our little church had no budget for decorations that year, but we were able to bum some leftover Christmas trees from a couple of local stores. We banked those trees in staggered heights behind the table holding the nativity scene at the front of the church and decorated the trees with what we had. That Christmas surely looked and felt real.

I decided that in the cool weather, I could save some of those branches that I was trimming off. It had been a while since our home had smelled of such a real thing of Christmas.

I almost had to be bonged on the *cabeza* by an evergreen branch to be reminded that with Christmas, it's better to just keep it simple, stupid.

When Christmas Went to the Dogs

No kind deed is wasted, not even on a stray, and that is most especially true on the eve of Christmas Day.

A diorama of days profound
  Was set upon the village church ground,
An open-fronted, rude barn of wood,
  Around which plaster shepherds stood.

Played on a stage of yellow wheat straw
  A Christmas scene was what passers saw
Of Mary, Joseph and the newborn King,
  And Magi, who rich gifts did bring.

Not unlike ancient starlit nights
  Were strings of twinkling colored lights
Laced through the trees around the site
  To wondrously illuminate the night.

Fitting sound for this scene of wonder
  Came from the steeple over yonder,
Where church bells rang forth the chimes
  Of joy, and cheer and goodwill times.

Even on the most frosty eve,
  There was a warmth here, to receive,
From being near, and glancing on,
  This scene reflecting days bygone.

When cold winds howled o'er their head,
  Stray dogs would sometimes find a bed
Amid the creche hay, a welcoming,
  Warm escape from winter's sting.

But church folk got irate, you see,
  About mutts invading their nativity,
With shouts and stones, they'd drive away
  Fleabitten interlopers in the manger hay.

"Out, you mutt, you mangy hound,
  We don't want your kind around,
We don't want no dog 'round here
  To desecrate our Christmas cheer."

Then came the eve of Christmas night,
  And all the stars were shining bright.
Carols were sung of holy birth,
  Great goodwill and peace on earth.

Outside the church an old cur dog passed,
  His days had been a lifelong fast.
Was plain to see, the little there
  Was mostly skin, and bones and hair.

The dog sought shelter from the night,
  His dim eyes spied the creche's light,
This outcast found a place to stay,
  And piled in midst the manger's hay.

He hunkered there to meekly await
  How this night would touch his fate.
A fitting place for an outcast stray,
  This rude stable and bed of hay.

The old dog kept good company,
  Ox, ass, lamb and the poor Family
Who found this lowly place to stay
  When the inns had all turned them away.

A kindly boy, now did pass,
 Hurrying to serve at midnight Mass.
The boy saw that the creche was blessed
 With an unexpected, lowly guest.

The old dog's eyes were brown and wide,
 He cowered to turn the kick aside,
The one he knew would come his way,
 On this, like any other day.

But the boy looked down with deep pity,
 For he too had once been cold and hungry,
He knew that many would feel no cheer
 Should they find this cur dog lying here.

"Rest well, my friend," the young boy said,
 Knelt down, rubbed the old dog's head,
And bunched close the bedding hay,
 To turn the cold night air away.

A gathering crowd expressed the mood:
 A dog in the manger is just no good,
"We don't want no dog 'round here
 To clutter-up our Christmas cheer."

They searched about for stones to throw
 Because that mangy mutt must go.
The boy sprawled across the cur, alone,
 And took the blow from the first stone.

Blood trickling from his wounded head,
 The boy turned to the crowd, and said,
" You poor people, can't you see
 This old dog's just the same as me?

"He wanted only some respite,
  Some place of peace on this holy night.
You took me in, so why can't you
    Have a care for this old stray dog, too?

"Is this any way to treat
  A guest lying at the Savior's feet?
Is it right, on eve of Christmas day,
  To turn a meek, mild guest away?

The crowd, they were all shamed to tears.
  Offering apologies, they drew near.
The old dog rose up from his bed
  And licked his new friend's wounded head.

They all rushed off home to find
  Such things as treat an old dog kind.
Table scraps and blankets too,
  They knew it was the right thing to do.

Midnight mass got started late,
  But no one seemed to mind the wait,
Nor when the well-fed dog did sing,
  When the Christmas bells began to ring.

Now, today in the parish, that boy is priest,
  He often sets stray dogs a feast,
And offers these wayfarers room to stay
  Amidst the rude old creche's hay.

And when he celebrates midnight Mass,
  Amidst the ringing, pealing brass,
You'll often hear a choir canine
  Join in caroling the night divine.

A Wrinkle in the Twinkle

At Christmas we can see the light—but only if we have the might—to smooth the wrinkle in the twinkle.

To celebrate this Christmas season
  Let's leave our senses—abandon reason,
To help us fully celebrate,
  Let's get outside and decorate!

Get on that roof and string the lights
  —Let's get them up before Christmas night.
If we get started right away,
  We can turn them on for Turkey Day.

We need new strings of sparkle lights,
  Last year's are just not working right
They're blowing fuses—there's a wrinkle
  These lights of Christmas just won't twinkle.

Go to the store and get new ones bought
  Before they're gone—and we're distraught.
Remember how it was last year?
  Not a light left in stores around here.

Off to the store, don't dillydally
  Get there first, elbow-out Aunt Sally!
To be the very first in line
  To buy the lights that make Christmas shine.

New lights bought and we've returned,
  Only to discover we have been burned,
Here's another lovely Christmas wrinkle
  These new lights—they still don't twinkle.

To decorate is your ambition,
  But you are surely no lighting technician.
As you discover, with a sheepish grin
  Lights twinkle great—if you plug them in.

Get on that roof, don't hesitate,
  We have a house to decorate.
Don't worry if that ladder sways,
  Just get up there before Christmas day.

On the roof, you slip and slide,
  Stringing lights on every side
The dogs are barking, they want up here,
  They'd love to tangle your Christmas cheer.

It's cold up here upon the roof,
  Your fumbling fingers try not to goof
And cause a whole string to lose its glow
  By crashing onto the driveway below.

You string a mile of extension cord,
  Wondering if there is some reward
For guys who play the Christmas clown—
  Putting up lights, then taking them down.

Finally, the roof is done,
  One skirmish of the battle's won,
You move on to the porch and hedges,
  Stringing lights around all the edges.

You keep checking the view from the street,
  Making sure that the job's complete,
Dadburn, this string won't work at all—
  It's missing a light, where did it fall?

The porch is done, the bushes, too,
　There's not a thing for you to do
But move on to the driveway tree,
　And deck it out flamboyantly.

Things look better, the spirit's stirring,
　Then you think about the meter whirring,
Christmas comes but once a year
　And to light this one up, you will pay dear.

Everybody look, the decor's so neat,
　Our holiday lighting scene is complete,
As we all revel in this view-of-views—
　Omigosh! We've blown a fuse!

Following the Stars

In a moment of aloneness a tractor driver witnesses the twinkling of hope against an indigo night sky.

The throaty thrum of the diesel engine and the glow of the fuel and amp, temp, oil pressure and tachometer gauges of the tractor's panel were company to him. Lights mounted on the cab and fenders stabbed into the darkness, illuminating the rutted county road.

He had finally gotten to that place where he had hoped to be a good month earlier—dumping the last load off the boll buggy into the module builder in a cloud of lint and dust.

Finishing up the last field had left him on the far side of the place. He had to road the rig down the turnrows and over to the other farm where he had left his pickup about mid-morning. A man could not stand to be parted from his pickup for long out in farm country. The shop and office-on-wheels held paperwork and tools, baling wire and duct tape—virtually the entire life support system for a farmer.

He should have been finished with cotton harvest long ago, but the fickle Plains weather had more than lived up to its reputation as this year wound down.

Suitable harvesting days had come only in short clusters this fall, frequently interrupted by rain and drizzle—that very same stuff that had been all but impossible to come by in the long-ago summer months, when this crop looked as if it would be a gin-buster.

All of the damp weather after the bolls had opened had taken a lot of the shine off of those prospects. The time of gathering that held such promise back in October had dragged on well into the days of December.

He counted himself lucky to have worked with a good crew of neighbors who took everything in stride—the breakdowns, the flats, tumbleweed-induced ball-ups and the rotten luck with the weather.

They rode it out and bore down and got the work done the best they could—nothing anybody could do about weather.

Rumbling along in road gear at partial throttle, the tractor had a rocking motion as the lugs of the tires bit the road. He glanced back periodically to check that the boll buggy wasn't bouncing excessively and tended his steering as he stared ahead. His mind raced with relief and played back the work and obstacle-clearing that had gone before.

He couldn't begin to count all of the late evenings he had spent here in this tractor cab in the last month. Winter days disappeared fast when the sun plunged spectacularly from the western sky and darkness enveloped everything outside of the dust-dimmed beam of tractor and cotton stripper lights.

They all worked as much as they could, when the weather would let them. Thanksgiving had come and gone in a blur. Christmas was coming fast. He felt in the midst of the hectic hurry of harvest, that he was missing the holiday.

Tooling down the road, surrounded by the darkness of the countryside, his glances over the gauges reminded him of Christmas tree lights. He thought on the glowing yellow-and-green bubblers, the glass balls and the clumped icicles that decorated the tree in the living room when he was growing up. He remembered how excited he was—so excited it was hard for him to sleep—when the big tree was being decked out by his parents. He would get to help put on the clingy icicles in great gobs.

To the drone of the diesel, he wondered to himself if, in this hurry-up world, little kids could still feel magic in this season.

Finally, the lights picked up the outline of his pickup and he wheeled the rig up alongside, idled the engine down, then shut off the lights and cut the ignition.

The sudden silence was deafening. He felt strangely alone in the darkness.

Gingerly, he opened the cab door, rose from the tractor seat and carefully felt his way down the steps with his feet.

On the ground, he stood for a moment next to the big tractor tire, letting his eyes adjust to what seemed an imposing darkness.

In that moment of aloneness, far out in the countryside, his eyes slowly absorbed not the inkiness of a dark night, but a great sweeping expanse of twinkling hope against the indigo sky.

He had been so busy worrying about things down here that he had not taken the time to look upward into the night for who knew how long?

Now, standing alone, his breath visible on the chill air, he shivered in amazement at the heavens adorned in their timeless Christmas best. Like the kid of years ago, he felt excitement and wonder. Here he was, small and insignificant—yet the stars shone over him with a glory as ancient as the Christmas story.

Finally, he climbed into the pickup. He started the motor, then dialed the cell phone.

"Honey? Yep, I just finished up. Hey, put on your coat right now and go outside and look at the sky. It's amazing. Have you and the kids finished decorating the tree? Would you wait for me? I'm on my way. I'll just follow the Christmas stars."

(This was written as a Christmas column following the September 11, 2001 terrorist attacks in New York, Washington, D.C. and Pennsylvania)

Coming Home

We have great hope of always turning homeward
in this season of stars and steeple bells.

We plan, always, to turn homeward
in the time of stars
and steeple bells,
angel choirs
and red candles trimmed with greenery.
Home for Christmas, we vow to ourselves,
in a hopeful voice.

We seek out family and friends,
wanting those we hold most dear
gathered in close-knit company,
their peaceful, joyous faces
illuminated by the soft glow
of hundreds of flickering candles
lighted at Christmas Eve services.

We yearn to be there,
singing and rejoicing with them,
voices raised in earnest tribute
to the silent, holy night.
We long to hear the friendly preacher,
to be a part of the celebration,
to feel the goodwill flowing freely,
to give, and get, best wishes.

We want to join in the bustle
of decoration and preparation.
To be part of the cooking
of turkey and dressing,
gravy and bread, and pies,
and special holiday candies.

We crave the impossible warmth
of a meaningful holiday,
Yet, its significance is only fully appreciated
when we are away,
removed from the familiar,
everyday trappings of the season.

I'll be Home for Christmas,
Peace on Earth, good will to men,
the seasonal songs proclaim.
We accept the promise of familiar stanzas
as our own pledge.
Painfully, we realize
that many—too many—will not be home,
and our fragile peace and good will is fleeting,
when fickle men attempt its husbandry.

The death of innocents
in unspeakable tragedies and acts of war
is hard to reconcile with what we feel
in a season borne for peace's sake.
We know there are many
felled by senseless hatred,
claimed in defense of common good,
or nothing more than happenstance,
who will never be home for Christmas again.

The table, laden with holiday excess,
yet tinged in sorrow
for empty chairs,
voices now stilled.
We ask God's grace,
His divine embrace
of those dear souls
now gone home.

Hosts of our countrymen are at their posts
on the sea, in the air,
walking the ground,
in cold desert climes
half-a-world away,
and even within our communities
on their watches to keep us safe.
Duty-bound, they stand for us
though it means they cannot be home.

Yet we turn homeward, still,
holding up those who are absent
with love, with remembrance.
Praying for their peace, their safe passage,
We are with them, if only in spirit,
in this season of coming home.

About the Author

JIM STEIERT grew up on an irrigated crop and livestock farm between the rural villages of Hart and Nazareth in Castro County, in the Texas Panhandle. A graduate of Hart High School, he attended West Texas State University, where he received a Bachelor of Science degree in journalism. After a stint in newspaper writing at the *Castro County News* in Dimmitt, Texas, and *The Hereford Brand* at Hereford, Texas, he served as associate editor of *The Texas Farmer-Stockman* magazine for 10 years. He has free-lanced as an agriculture and outdoor writer for nearly 30 years, and has contributed articles to numerous outdoor magazines including *Texas Parks & Wildlife*. He resides in Hereford, where he is the editor of *The Co-Op Connection*, the newsletter of West Texas Rural Telephone Cooperative. He has written his rural-based column "On the Turnrow," recipient of a National Newspaper Association column-writing award, for over 20 years. He has received numerous writing awards from the Texas Outdoor Writers Association. *Country Turnrows* is his second book. His first, *Playas: Jewels of the Plains*, published by Texas Tech University Press, is a natural history of the playa lakes of the Southern High Plains, and was named a Texas Outdoor Writers Association *Outdoor Book of the Year*.